W9-BJN-105

MORNING
has
BROKEN

Murphey Candler Wilds

MORNING
has
BROKEN

FURTHER
MEDITATIONS
ON THE
LIFE OF
CHRIST

Providence House Publishers
PROVIDENCE PUBLISHING CORPORATION
FRANKLIN, TENNESSEE

Copyright 2004 by Murphey Candler Wilds

All rights reserved. Written permission must be secured from the publisher to use or reproduce any part of this book, except for brief quotations in critical reviews or articles.

Printed in the United States of America

08   07   06   05   04   1   2   3   4   5

Library of Congress Control Number: 2004102982

ISBN: 1-57736-318-3

Cover art by Murphey Candler Wilds
Cover design by Kelly Bainbridge and Gary Bozeman

Quote on page 30 by an unknown author.

PROVIDENCE HOUSE PUBLISHERS
an imprint of
Providence Publishing Corporation
238 Seaboard Lane • Franklin, Tennessee 37067
www.providence-publishing.com
800-321-5692

To
Sue Garrett Treas,
whose generosity
of spirit, time, and talents
has made this book possible

PREVIOUS WORKS

Songs in the Night:
Meditations on the Life of Christ

Contents

> They Borrowed a Manger to Lay Him In, 206 • He Borrowed a Bed to Lay His Head, 206 • He Borrowed Some Loaves and Some Fish, 206 • He Borrowed a Donkey to Ride Upon, 207 • He Borrowed a Room on a Thursday Night, 207 • He Borrowed a Garden Across a Brook, 207 • They Borrowed a Cross to Crucify Him, 207 • They Borrowed the Strength of a Stranger From Cyrene, 208 • They Borrowed a Tomb When He Had Died, 208

Acknowledgments

As I complete this second book of meditations on the life of Christ, I acknowledge again the strong Christian faith instilled in me by my parents, Laura Candler and Louis Trezevant Wilds.

In my fifty-six years of marriage to Mary Rose Mitchener Wilds, I have been supported by her deep faith and love for our Lord. We have been companions and partners during my seven pastorates and retirement in the Presbyterian Church (USA). Through these years we have shared in the joy and love brought to us by our children, Scott, Martin, Mitch, and Ferne and our grandchildren, Alex and Sarah. God has blessed us and been gracious to us all.

May you who read this book find his grace and peace through Jesus Christ our Lord.

MORNING
has
BROKEN

The Creed of the Church

I Believe in God
Matthew 6:25-34

The Christian church has been a confessional
church from its earliest days—confessional,
not in the sense in which
we often use the word,
an admission, with sadness,
of sin and wrongdoing,
but confessional in the sense
of confidence and certainty and
willingness to take a stand.

In a confession of its faith, the church says:
"This we believe, regardless
of what others may believe
or of any hardship
which may come to us
for taking this stand."

As the early church spread
through the Roman empire,
groups of Christians in various localities
developed their own statements of faith.

There was a great variety of wording,
    yet an amazing agreement of ideas.
Gradually, these local creeds were written down
    and combined into a single form.
This was the course of the creed
    most often used in our day, the Apostles' Creed.

Without the calling of any council or any vote
    this creed reached its present form
        in the sixth or seventh century
            and became dominant in the church
                in the eighth century.
The apostles themselves had nothing to do with it,
    though it carries us back closer than any other
        to the faith of the church immediately
            following the apostles.

This is the creed we use most often during worship
    in a congregation of Christ's people.

It makes no effort to prove God,
    to set forth any of the common arguments
        which might be made
            as to the existence of God.
In this it follows the Scriptures,
    which begin with the simple statement:
        "In the beginning God . . ."

Far more important for us
    than such proofs or arguments
        is the fact that others and we
            have been led to understand
                and have experienced that God
                    has a way of slipping into human life.

What kind of God is he?
This is where the creed begins.

The first part of its answer is in the words:
    "I believe in God the Father Almighty,
        Maker of heaven and earth."

Three beliefs are offered here.
If we look at them in reverse order,
    we do so in the sequence
        in which God revealed himself to us.

First, I believe in God,
    Maker of heaven and earth,
        all that is in the heavens above,
        all that is on the earth beneath.

This would say particularly to us,
    who are human and deeply concerned
        about human life,
            that he is the giver of life to us.

So far as his method of creation,
    neither the creed nor the Scriptures
      are greatly concerned.

We encounter many difficulties
    when we attempt to make the Bible
      answer how God called into being all that is.
The answer is not intended to be there.
The Bible is a book about God and man.
It is a theological textbook, not a scientific
    textbook.

So the creation accounts of Genesis
    allow room for different ideas
      as to how God worked.

With the point being that
    behind everything that is, is God,
      using whatever method he chose.

At the beginning, and before, there is God,
    without whom nothing was made that was made.

The second point made in this article of the creed
    is: I believe in God Almighty.

The Maker of heaven and earth is almighty.
He remains in control of all he created.

He did not bring all that is into being
    and then cast any part of it loose.
He maintained his responsibility for
    authority over his creation.

Of course we admit humankind is not
    as God created it.
For God created us with freedom to choose,
    to follow his will or go our own way.
We exercised our freedom in such a way
    as to go against God's design.

Yet, when we say we believe in God Almighty,
    we are saying that, despite our sin,
        God still is capable of working out
            his purpose for humankind.

The Old Testament parable of the potter
    and the clay makes this clear.
Impurities in the clay, as in the life of men
    and women, destroy the design.
Yet the potter still has everything in hand.
He kneads the clay until the impurity is removed,
    sets it back on the wheel,
        and works his will upon it.
He is stronger and greater than the clay.

When we say, "I believe in God Almighty,"
      we are saying we believe in a God
         who will do this with the world.
Even at this moment of history, or any other,
      "though the wrong seem oft so strong,
            God is the ruler yet."
The third point to keep before ourselves
      in this article of the creed is:
            I believe in God the Father.

This one who is Maker of heaven and earth,
      this one who is almighty,
            has a father's heart and a father's way.

This changes our outlook on the other two parts
      of the statement.
What if God were some monstrous,
      evil creator intent on working out his will?
Thomas Hardy finished his novel
      telling of the troubled and tortured
            life of Tess with these words
                  "The President of the Immortals
                        had finished his sport with Tess."

He is our Father! What a difference!

This descriptive term for God, Father,
      had been used only sparingly
            before Jesus walked this earth.

Jesus brought this into the spotlight
      and it became the focal point
            of his teachings about God.
Pray: "Our Father . . ."

Not that Jesus has given us a picture
      of an indulgent father, granting his children
            all they wish and ask for,
                  endlessly pampering them.
Rather, his is a higher concept of a father
      who can be stern when that is needed,
            but stern in love,
                  of a father who seeks and works
                        for his children's good
                              rather than for what his children
                                    think is best.

And then, I believe in God the Father Almighty,
      Maker of heaven and earth.

So what?

This can only be answered by the understanding
      that belief falls short,
            that only faith is enough,
                  faith beyond belief
                        to a commitment based on that belief.

Faith is belief in action.
Faith is a gift of God's grace,
    not something we can obtain for ourselves,
        no matter how hard we try.

Belief turned faith is living beneath an acceptance
    of God's creation and might.
Faith means living aware of the fact that
    the outcome of our lives is not in our hands
        but in his hands.
Faith is to live under the surety
    that God is in control
      and will in his own time, in his own way,
        work life out according
           to a loving Father's design.

Sidney Lanier describes such faith in these words
    from "The Marshes of Glynn":

"As the marsh-hen builds on the watery sod. . .
    I will build me a nest on the greatness of God."

Again, belief turned to faith means
    receiving from God the power
        to become the children of God
           he meant us to be.
It is to reach out and accept
    what he holds out to us.

With this, faith involves acceptance
    of God's intention to unite us
        in one family, the family of God.

"I believe in God the Father Almighty,
    Maker of heaven and earth."
The outcome of this belief in terms of faith is:
    trust the mighty Father who made us,
        and live as his children.

I Believe in Jesus Christ

The Apostles' Creed begins in the heights.
Not the heights geographically,
    but the heights of power and glory.
"I believe in God the Father Almighty,
    Maker of heaven and earth."
At this point, the creed takes us
    on a downward journey,
        a steep descent from the heights
            to the depths of being.
Then, just as surely,
    from the depths there is a movement
        upward to the heights.

All this takes place in the second section
    of the creed:
"I believe in Jesus Christ his only Son our Lord,"
The downward journey begins with the incarnation,
    a word coming from two Latin words:
        in, and flesh, enfleshed.

At a certain point in history, God Almighty,
   Maker of heaven and earth,
      was enfleshed and became a human being.
We know God through his creation.
We live in a world which reflects
   his wisdom and his power.
We know God through the insight
   and writings of historians
     who have seen God at work
       in the affairs of human beings.
We know God through the work of the prophets
   whose insight was so sharpened
     that they could voice his will.

But we know him fully and perfectly
   only in Jesus Christ,
     God enfleshed,
      God become man,
       God become one of us.

The creed expresses it:
   "was conceived by the Holy Ghost,
     born of the virgin Mary."
Strangely enough we have often
   turned these phrases around
     from their original purpose.
The creed came into being during a period
   in which the idea of the divinity of Christ

was not threatened, but the idea
of the humanity of Christ was.
The creed contradicted the idea that God
was not really, all the way,
a human being, a man,
that he would not descend
to such a state as to really be
one of us.

In answer, the Apostles' Creed states that
he was born of a woman as all human beings.
This is the emphasis of the statement.

To be sure, we should not be surprised
that there is here a statement
of wondrous circumstances
when God became a human being.

If, as the creed states,
Jesus Christ was God Almighty
become one of us, we should not wonder
at mysterious and unfamiliar facets
of that happening.
It is not inconceivable that a unique person
should have a unique beginning:
"conceived by the Holy Ghost,
born of the Virgin Mary."

This was the first step in the downward journey,
    the Creator's becoming one of us.
This happened at a specific point in human history.
It could have happened at any moment.
But the life of God in human form
    is tied down to a particular time
        and a particular place.
He lived and walked about in the world
    when Pontius Pilate was the Roman governor
        of Judea.

Under that governor,
    in that time and place,
        he suffered.

This was another step in the downward journey
    of the maker of Heaven and Earth
        into the fullest life of his creatures.
His suffering centered about crucifixion,
    the means of execution reserved
        for the most debased criminal.
And the consequence of crucifixion was death,
    with that which follows death, burial.

The creed then states, "He descended into Hell."

What does the phrase mean?

There are two primary interpretations
    which Reformed theology has made in answer.
One of these is in *The Westminster Confession*:
"Christ's humiliation after his death
    consisted in his being buried,
        continuing in a state of the dead,
            under the power of death
                till the third day, which has otherwise
                been expressed in these words,
                    'he descended into hell.'"

The *Confession* recognizes that "hell"
    as used in the creed is the word
        used by the Bible to connote
        the state of being dead.
So the creed underscores what has gone before.
He was really dead, no doubt about it.
This in answer to those who have said
    through history that he was not really dead,
    but only appeared to be.

This statement avers there was no fakery here,
    no sleight of hand.
This was not a hoax.
He really died.

A second helpful interpretation
    of the phrase is that of John Calvin:

"The deepest suffering was not in the nails,
        but in the suffering expressed
            by his sense of being forsaken by his Father,
                being cut off from him,
                    an inner suffering of heart
                        and mind and spirit."
Calvin was saying, as we do today
    of certain experiences of life,
        "He went through hell!"

So the end of the downward journey—
    the very depths of human experience,
        dead, cut off from the loving Father.

And now begins a statement of a journey upward,
    of a glorious movement
        in the opposite direction.
It began on the third day after the crucifixion.

The creed affirms: "on the third day
    he rose again from the dead."

Death could not hold him.
    Why should we wonder at this, after saying,
        "I believe in God the Father Almighty."
Almighty!
God is stronger even than death.
This gospel of the resurrection was the central
    theme of the proclamation of the early Christians.

They spoke of Christ's crucifixion and death, yes.
But the "good news" they proclaimed
   was that of the empty tomb
     and of a power greater than death.
They preached a victorious, living Lord,
   not a defeated, dead one.

And the upward movement goes on,
   not upward geographically so much
     as in a state of being.
He ascended into heaven from the depths
   to the heights!
The ascension was also a landmark
   in that it was the ending of the way
    of his being with his followers
      in which his physical presence was visible,
     and the beginning of his being
       with them in a different way.

Human beings have limitations placed upon them.
So did the man Jesus.

When God became man
   he imposed upon self certain limitations.
He was limited by time and space.
He was not at all times present everywhere.
When he was in Galilee
   he was not in Jerusalem.

His ascension marks the removal
    of all such limitations.
"And sitteth on the right hand
    of God the Father Almighty."
The creed intends this to be a symbol
    of authority and power,
        the completion of the journey
            downward and upward.
Martin Luther said that the right hand
    of God is everywhere.
Calvin wrote: "when Christ is said
    to be in heaven, we must not view him
        as dwelling among the spheres.
The phrase simply means he is the active,
    reigning Lord of all."

One last statement is made here
    about him in the creed,
        speaking of what is to be.
"From thence he shall come
    to judge the quick and the dead,"
        (the living and the dead).
This speaks of the fact he continues
    to be involved in our lives,
        and will meet us at the end
            of human life and at the end
            of human history.

At the end there will be the God
　　we have come to know in Jesus Christ.
Those who know him could desire no other judge.
So we say, "I believe in Jesus Christ,
　　his only Son, our Lord."

But what of faith, thinking again of faith
　　as belief in action,
　　as belief doing something?

Up to this point in the creed
　　　the expressed belief regarding Jesus Christ
　　　　is that in him the mighty maker
　　　　　descended in a downward journey,
　　　　　ascended in an upward journey,
　　　　　　and has every right to be Lord,
　　　　　　　the supreme authority in life.

It is not until later that we come
　　to the theme of Jesus Christ as Savior.
It is much easier to act on the belief that Jesus
　　is Savior than on the belief that Jesus is Lord.

The action of belief in Jesus as Savior
　　involves taking, accepting, receiving.

The action of belief in Jesus as Lord
　　involves giving, submission, obedience.

Belief in Jesus as Lord becomes faith
   as we recognize he has every right
      to be just that, as we surrender our wills,
         our desires, all that we are and have to him,
         withholding nothing.
So right here within the Apostles' Creed
   is the earliest, shortest creed of the church:
      Jesus is Lord.

Belief which has become faith is to abandon
   any thought that "I am the master of my fate,
     I am the captain of my soul,"
       and to live under the Lordship
        of Jesus Christ.

So let every tongue confess and sing that
   Jesus Christ is Lord!

I Believe in the Holy Ghost

1 Corinthians 12:14–13:3

"I believe in the Holy Ghost,"
    we say in the Apostles' Creed.
In some ways it is unfortunate
    we still use the word "Ghost."
For it has an echo of haunted houses
    and mysterious apparitions.
It is the Saxon word for "Spirit."
And with that we may feel
    more comfortable.

The idea of "spirits" has existed
    in almost all civilizations.
The Hebrews had a word for it:
    ruach, which means wind.
The Greeks had a word for it:
    pneuma, which means breath.

Some ancient one first noted that
    when death came to another,
        there was no longer a wind
            or a breath coming from that other.

Something which was at the center of life,
   which was life, was no longer present.
Whatever that mysterious, invisible force
   symbolized by the breath was,
      surely it was greater than the body.

For without it, the body disintegrated
   and was no longer.

It was not a great leap from this to the idea
   that man has a spirit,
      or to the Christian idea that man
         is a spirit and has a body.
The spirit is man in essence.

When we speak of the Holy Spirit, we are saying
      there is a Spirit distinct from and apart
         from the spirits of human beings.

We have already said in the creed:
   "I believe in God the Father Almighty,
      maker of heaven and earth;
         and in Jesus Christ his only Son our Lord."

We are familiar with the human relationships
   upon which these concepts are based.
It is more difficult for us to conceive
   of God as the Holy Spirit,

for there is no human relationship
to hold beside that other than
the idea of our spirits clothed
in human bodies.
Perhaps that is enough.
The Old Testament tells us the Spirit
of the Lord clothed himself with Gideon.

But even more difficult is it to think
of God the Father, Son, and Holy Spirit
while holding to the basic belief
of Hebrew and Christian theology
that there is only one God.
If we could go with three gods, it would be easier.
But we cannot.
It is counter to God's revelation of himself.

Many explanations of this which have been given
have been just as wrong as that of three gods.

There was the subordination scheme, that
the Father is superior to the Son
and the Holy Spirit, both being
subordinate to him.

There was the modalism scheme, that at one time
God showed himself as the Father,
then canceled that out

and showed himself as the Son,
then canceled that out
and showed himself as the Holy Spirit.

The only way the church has been able
to say it is "trinity."
Tri-unity—God—three in one.
God: Father, Son, Holy Spirit, all equal.
God: Father, Son, Holy Spirit,
all at the same time.

This is the church's answer to the experience
of human beings with God as described
in the Scriptures.
Let us admit this is too much
for our minds to comprehend and explain.

God has dealt with us as God over us,
our Maker and Ruler, our Father.
God has dealt with us as God with us,
in the midst of our earthly existence,
our redeemer and the revealer of the Father,
in Jesus Christ his Son.
And God has dealt with us as God within us,
giving us new life and power
through the Holy Spirit
to become what he would have us be.

Most of us have tried to come up
   with some explanation of the Trinity.
Whatever it is, it must maintain the oneness of God
   while allowing for the distinctions
     of Father, Son, and Holy Spirit.
It is at this point that the contemporary
   "Holy Spirit" movement comes to mind.
Variously called the "neo-Pentecostal" or
"charismatic" movement, its excesses
    present some very real dangers.

One of these is that it sometimes tends
   to ignore the idea of the Trinity,
    coming very close to offering
     a theology of tritheism, or three gods.

It makes the Holy Spirit more important
   than the others of the Trinity.
It speaks of the Holy Spirit far more frequently,
   almost excessively and exclusively.
It sees the Holy Spirit as making distinctive gifts
   apart from the Father and the Son.
This is the subordination heresy in reverse.

There is also lurking around the idea
   that the Father sent the Son;
    the Son came and died, rose from the dead,
     and returned to the Father;

and that Father and Son are somewhere
off yonder in semi-retirement
while the only one present with us
now is the Holy Spirit.
This is the modalism heresy.

God is one.
The Holy Spirit is the Spirit of the Father,
is the Spirit of the Son,
not some separate and distinct being.

It is God we are dealing with
and who is dealing with us,
not one of three gods,
not a third of one God.

"The Scriptures affirm the unity
of God's being and work.

We may not separate the work of God as Creator
from the work of God as Redeemer.

We may not set the Son's love
against the Father's justice.
We may not value the Holy Spirit's work
above the work of the Father and Son.
Father, Son and Holy Spirit are one God."

Another danger of the contemporary movement
    centering upon the Holy Spirit is that it involves,
        quite frequently, a topsy-turvy interpretation
            of what is noted as being "gifts of the spirit"
            and which are offered as proof
                that one is "spirit-filled."
Though there are others presented,
        the "gift" most frequently held up
            and talked about as exceedingly desirable
                is that of speaking in unknown tongues,
                    or glossalalia.

Now one must always interpret the Scriptures
        by the Scriptures themselves.
This surely is a case in point.

In his letter to the church at Corinth,
        Paul points out that God gives
            many different kinds of gifts
                to many different people in the church,
                    not the same gifts to all people.

In the list of gifts Paul names "speaking in tongues,"
        but he puts this at the end of the list.

The neo-Pentecostal or charismatic movement
        in our time has reversed the order,
            listing Paul's unimportant gift as being first.

Further, Paul goes on to point out that no gift
    is anything unless it is accompanied
        by the highest and most excellent gift, love.

This was the whole purpose of Paul's writing
    this part of the letter.
Those in Corinth were to recognize a diversity
    of abilities and functions.
They were not to use these, as some had been doing,
    to form elite groups who looked down on others.

They were to build up the community in love,
    and to equip it for its mission in the world.

This immediately makes us see another warning flag.
This is that over and again
    the neo-pentecostal movement has often contributed
        disunity to the church rather than unity.

Congregations have been torn apart
    by those concentrating on misvalued
        gifts who say in effect to those
            who make no claim to them,
                and have no desire to do so:
"You are not a person in whom
    the Spirit of God dwells.

You must have this gift,
    or you have been left out."

So the Holy Spirit, whom Jesus points out as
    the great unifier, is made
        into the great disunifier,
            one who brings disorder and disharmony
                rather than peace and unity in love.

The Holy Spirit unified the church,
    binding those with tensions and conflicts
        into one body enriched by their differences.

The Holy Spirit moves among us
    not to end diversity or compel uniformity
        but to overcome divisiveness and bitterness.

If the opposite comes about on the part of some,
    there is something seriously wrong with their
        concept of the Spirit of God and his work
            with and in individuals and congregations.

One last warning signal to hoist is that
    the present day "Holy Spirit" movement
        centers faith in feelings and emotions
            and ecstatic experiences.

Dr. Donald Miller wrote:
"Life cannot be constantly keyed up
    to transporting emotional levels
        without ultimately destroying the person.

Although mind, feelings, and will,
    it relates more to the will
        than to the feelings.
The (Christian) faith involves not so much
    emotional states as moral decision,
        commitment, trust, duty, service, obedience.
The ecstasy of the mount of transfiguration
    cannot be sustained, nor should it be.
Life leads to the tragedies at the foot
    of the mountain, and to the day-by-day
        demands of steady living."

Tied to the emotions only,
    faith as presented by the present-day movement,
        frequently tends to leave all solutions
            to the problems and tragedies of daily life
            to direct interventions of God.

"God will work out the problem
    if faith is great enough.
If he does not, then faith
    was not what it should have been."

So the movement makes light of the fact
    that the way God has most often worked
        in human affairs has been
            through the gift of human minds

to work on human problems
    with the resources he has placed in the world.
For most times, and for most people,
    God gives minds and resources
        which he intends us to use
            rather than to sit back
                and to count on "miracles".

"I believe in God the Father Almighty,
    Maker of heaven and earth . . .
And in Jesus Christ his only Son our Lord . . .
I believe in the Holy Spirit . . ."
    God so very near he is within us,
        perfecting what has been begun in us.

How do you know he is within you?
    You don't have to speak in tongues
        or give others exotic evidences.

If you believe in Christ, that is evidence enough
    that you have the Holy Spirit.
Paul wrote: "No one can say 'Jesus is Lord'
    except by the Holy Spirit."
If life is submitted to Jesus Christ as Lord,
    that is the basic, most certain sign.

And, if certain results are growing within your life,
    that is evidence that you have the Spirit of God.

Again Paul wrote: "The fruit of the Spirit is love,
joy, peace, patience, kindness, goodness,
faithfulness, gentleness, self-control."
These are the gifts to be most desired.
"And the greatest of these is love."

I Believe in the Holy Catholic Church

Matthew 16:13–20; Ephesians 4:1–6

Imagine many, many people,
    scattered throughout an area
      in homes and places of work and play,
        holding to varying ideals
        and senses of values,
        having little contact with each other,
        having few common interests,
          suddenly being called
            by every possible means: "Come!"

They drop whatever they are doing.
They leave the desk, the kitchen sink,
    the ballpark, the shop, the classroom,
      and move to some designated place
        to assemble for whatever purpose
          was in the mind of the one
            who summoned them.

Imagine this, and you have the meaning
    of the Greek word, *ecclesia,*
      which we translate "church."

In the New Testament, the church is seen
    as an assembly of people
      called from where they are
        and from what they have been doing,
        called by God for his purposes.

We are called to worship him.
The God we have come to experience
    as Father, Son, and Holy Spirit
      is by all means worthy
        of adoration and praise.
This is so by reason of who he is
    and what he has done:
      our Maker, which means we are his creatures.
He has redeemed us and he sustains us.

We are called to be a certain kind of people.
We are to live in a certain way
    as a people whose life together
      is patterned after his design.

So living together, we are to reflect
    his glory to the world,
      which is, in itself, a form of worship.

We are called to share the good news about him.
We are "a chosen race, a royal priesthood,
    a holy nation, God's own people,
      that we may declare the wonderful deeds

of him who called us out of darkness
into his marvelous light."
And we are called to serve him.
Service is a form of worship
and cannot be separated from worship.
In the New Testament, God's people are seen
as being called not simply
that they may be saved
but that they may serve.
They are called for responsibility,
not only for privilege.

It is significant that he
who is to judge the quick and the dead
indicates in his description
of that judgment that the standard
for judgment is to be service or ministry.
"Come, O blessed of my Father,
inherit the kingdom prepared for you
from the foundation of the world; for
I was hungry and you gave me food.
I was thirsty and you gave me drink.
I was a stranger and you welcomed me,
I was naked and you clothed me,
I was sick and you visited me,
I was in prison and you came to me.
As you did it to one of the least of these,
my brethren, you did it to me."

This people called out by God,
 the church, we say in the creed, is holy.
We may not be quite sure about this.
We know the church.
We know the congregation of which we are part.
And we must confess that this word "holy"
 is not always appropriate to describe us.

Through the ages the church has often
 taken stands and committed deeds
  which have not harmonized
   with the life and mind of Christ
    and which have not reflected
     his glory to the world.

If this is what holy means,
 we are not the holy church.
But this is not what holy means.

The church is holy in the sense
 that the word "holy" means separated,
  or different, or set apart.

The church is holy only in that it is God's church.
The Anglo-Saxon word "church" comes
 from a Greek word which means
  "belonging to the Lord."
In this sense it is holy.

The church belongs to God and is holy
    because he originated it,
    because he called it into being.
It was not constituted by people but by God.
So it is holy.

The church belongs to God and so is holy
    because he lives in it.
At Pentecost he came in his Spirit
    to fill the Christian community,
      to renew the church which had been old Israel,
        and make it into the new Israel
          by giving it his Spirit and a new life.

He continues to be in it.
He continues to be the source of its power.
He continues to work in and through it
    to do his will.
He is its very life.
So it is holy.

The church belongs to God, and so is holy,
    because he is its head.
The church is the body of Christ.
This is not a figurative expression only.
It is real.
The Lord is the head of the church,
    its supreme authority.

So it is holy.

These things can be said of no other institution
    or gathering or community of persons.
Name any in existence.
There is none that is holy,
    originated or created by God,
        indwelt or lived in by God,
            headed by God.

We also say of the church that it is catholic.

We should not avoid the word "catholic"
        because one branch of the church,
            the Roman Catholic Church,
                frequently abbreviates its name
                    and uses only the word "Catholic."

This word belongs to all of us
    and should not be neglected by any of us.
It means in essence "universal,"
    which includes the idea of unity or oneness.

We can understand this when
    we recall the fact that
        the church is the body of Christ,
            and his body cannot be divided.
His body was broken once, yes,
    but divided, separated into pieces, no, never.

The church is catholic
    because it has one Lord,
        one faith, one baptism,
            one God and Father of us all.
There are not many lords, not many faiths,
    not many baptisms, not many gods,
        only one.

This is so, despite appearances to the contrary.
Despite the divisions humans have caused,
    there is a unity they cannot destroy.
When we say, "I believe in the holy catholic church,"
    we are confessing that our congregation
        is not all there is to the church.

The one denomination is not
    all there is to it.
The Reformed faith and tradition are not
    all there is to it.
The Protestant branch is not all there is to it.
We are confessing that Jesus Christ transcends
    all ecclesiastical structures.
We belong to the church of Jesus Christ
    which knows no boundaries in space,
        even in time.
Those who live on the face
    of the earth today are part of it.
Those who have ever walked this earth
    are to be a part of it,

Peter, Paul, those who followed them,
        our own dear ones we no longer see,
                now part of the church triumphant,
        those of every place and nation
                and generation.
There is only one church:
        the Church Catholic,
        the Church Universal.

Faith is to take this belief and act upon it.
Faith is belief in action.

This belief becomes faith on the part of anyone
        who is deeply and fully involved
                in the worship and work of the church,
                        rather than standing on the sidelines.
It is to give self wherever and whenever
        and however the Lord of the church calls.

This belief becomes faith on the part of anyone
        who recognizes its holiness and
                sees the church as God's possession,
                as belonging to him rather than
                as his or her personal possession.

This belief becomes faith on the part of anyone
        who always rejoices at any sign
                of its oneness, and seeks and works

for increased evidence of unity
within its life.

As belief takes such actions
we can state with reality:
"I believe in the Holy Catholic Church."

I Believe in the Forgiveness of Sins

Romans 5:1–11

We are unique in creation.
We are the only creature
    who has rebelled against the Maker
        of heaven and earth,
            who has twisted and distorted
                God's grand design for us.

Only in us do we find sin, which means to miss
    the mark, the goal, the target as set by God.
The stars, the moon, the sun, the planets
    move unswervingly in their orbits.

Vegetation responds to moisture and light
    and warmth and grows and bears fruit.
The lower forms of animal life invariably
    act upon the instincts planted deep
        within them.

God's reaction to our sin might have taken
    any one of three courses.

The first might have been to exact
   the full penalty of sin.
No one could blame the Creator if he allowed us
    to receive the full consequences
      of our rebellion against him.
We do not blame others who exact penalties in life.

We expect officials of athletic contests
     to prescribe penalties against those
       who violate the rules.

We expect those responsible for the administration
     of justice to exact the penalty
       of those convicted of crimes.

We could not blame God if the consequences
   of our sins were placed upon us.
The law has been laid down,
    with this the final word:
      the wages of sin is death,
       the ultimate death,
         separation from God.

But this is not the course our heavenly Father chose.
Because he loves us he sought
    some other way of dealing with us
      than by punishing us according
        to our iniquities and rewarding us
          according to our transgressions.

The second course he might have chosen
     could have been to ignore our sins,
          so that when we sin,
               we would hear God say:
"That's all right. It really doesn't matter.
     Forget it!"

Some people do think
     this is God's attitude toward sin.
They look on him as a good-natured,
     broad-minded gentleman,
          quite eager and willing
               to overlook our faults and failures
                    and treat us as though
                         we had never sinned at all.

But God does not do this.
Sin does makes a difference.
To take this course would be
     to show an absence of love
          and concern for us.

When children do wrong,
     they must be disciplined
          for their own good.

The parent who smiles indulgently
     at a child's misbehavior is storing up
          for the day he will look at that child

become an adult, and see a person
quite different from the one
he had wanted the child to be.

So God, who is wisdom and goodness,
did not, by his very nature,
take that course, for our own good.

And God did not take that course
because of what the sins of one person
can do to other human beings.
Our Father has an obligation toward all his children.

Sin is like a stone dropped into the waters
of a quiet pool, causing ripples
to spread concentrically
until even the waters
at the very edge of the pond
are disturbed.
It is impossible for an individual to sin
and injure only himself.
If God paid no attention to sin,
he would not only encourage it,
but would also be an accomplice in the injuries
inflicted upon others by sin.

And God did not ignore sin
because of what he is in himself.

Here and there in human life
    we see individuals who cannot by their nature
        look upon certain human scenes
            without feelings of grief and revulsion.
They cannot see injustice, suffering and disease,
    for instance, and remain unaffected
        by what they see.

Human beings cannot remain unaffected
    by these sights.
How can God, whose being
    puts to shame the noblest of them,
        look upon that which is wholly incompatible
            with his nature and ignore it?

The third course open to God
    was the one taken:
        the forgiveness of sins.

Obviously there is a difference between
    the forgiveness of sins
        and allowing us to suffer
            the full effect of sin.
There is also a difference
    between the way of ignoring sin
        and the way of forgiveness,
            though the difference
                may not be as obvious.

In forgiveness part of the result of sin
      is removed, but not all.
The result which is removed
      is alienation or separation from God.

But other results very often remain in effect.
A person may misuse his or her body so that,
      by the time one is forty, it is that
            of a person many years older.
He may know the forgiveness of God for his sins,
      but he does not, with forgiveness,
            receive by parcel post a new body
                  in which he may live from
                        that moment on.
He must still live with the damage done
      to his body by his sins.

A person's sin may injure one of his fellows.
A speeding driver may kill a child.
But for him to experience the forgiveness of God,
      and even the forgiveness of the child's parents,
            does not bring that child back.
So the results of sin often continue
      and are not undone by forgiveness.

Edwin Lewis wrote:
      "To pray for forgiveness is to confess sin.
            It is to accept its consequences.

Only in one point do I ask
    that the consequences be lifted from me.
I ask that they no longer come between God
    and me.
I ask that I be treated by God as one
    between whom no barrier exists."

This is not just because God has said
    he will suspend this effect of sin.

It is because, as Paul put it:
    he bore our sins in his own body
        upon the tree.

We have already said in the creed,
"I believe in Jesus Christ, his only Son, our Lord."

The words there that tell us
    he was crucified, dead, and buried,
        coupled with this statement
            of belief in the forgiveness of sins,
                is to confess him as Savior
                as well as Lord.

So, God has not allowed that consequence of sin,
    which is separation from himself, to remain.

On the other hand, he has not ignored sin
    and so minimized its horror.

Only at the cost of his own life
    was the supreme consequence of sin removed.

Now it must be said that it is impossible
    for anyone to understand this fully.
The wonder of it is that we do not have
    to understand it fully to accept it,
        anymore than we have to understand fully
            the workings of an aircraft
                to be a passenger.
Rather, we accept what has been done
    by our Father through Jesus Christ
        his only Son as it has been revealed
            and authenticated by the Holy Spirit
            and by our own experience
                of restoration to God.

The forgiveness of sins is God's way
    with any person who in penitence and in faith
        seeks forgiveness through Christ.

In a book of quite some years ago,
    Echoes of Flanders, there is the story
        of an English soldier who had run away
            from home as a boy and gone
            from bad to worse,
                spending much time in prison.

In the army he was deemed to be utterly incorrigible
   by those of his regiment.
Finally one of the officers,
     as a last daring experiment,
        made the young man his personal orderly.
An almost magic transformation then took place.

In the end the soldier sacrificed his life
   for the officer whose trust had changed him.

As darkness fell after that battle,
    and his life slowly ebbed away,
       there came to this once worthless man,
         by some strange whim of memory,
            a prayer learned at his mother's knee
            and quite forgotten
               in the reckless years he had lived.
Now, gasping for breath, he began repeating it.
The stretcher bearers heard the words
   as of a tired child at the end of day:
     "The day is done, O God the Son,
      Look down upon thy little one.
      O light of light, keep me this night
      And shed around thy presence bright."

And on the scarred face of the man
   whom no one had loved for so long

there was a light like that of heaven;
    and the words were trailing off into silence,
    but the last ones came:

        "I need not fear if thou art near,
            Thou art my Savior, kind and dear.
            So happily and peacefully
                I lay me down to rest in thee."

Such is the forgiveness of sins.

I Believe in the Resurrection of the Body and the Life Everlasting

John 14:1–7

This statement of the Apostles' Creed
    centers upon Jesus Christ who was crucified
        dead and buried and who, on the third day,
            rose again from the dead.

It was the testimony of countless witnesses
    who knew Jesus that he had overcome death;
        that, though he had died, he still lived.

Further, he had said:
    "Because I live, you shall live also."
And he had said:
    "I am the resurrection and the life.
        He who believes in me, though he were dead,
            yet shall he live. And whoever lives
                and believes in me shall never die."

Thus the creed affirms the promises of Christ
    concerning the life that follows death.
While neither the creed nor the Scriptures

tell us all we would like to know
about the life everlasting, still enough
is given to enable Christ's people
to look beyond death
with hope and with joy.
We ask three questions about this.

The first is where shall we be after death?

In answer, there is John's description
of the new heaven and the new earth,
of the new Jerusalem, glorified
with its streets of gold
and its walls of jasper.

Yet, whereas these terms may have meant
much literally to those who were Jews
and lived in that age in old Jerusalem,
those of us who live today
are not overly impressed by them.

These are not the most important features
of the heaven seen by John,
or of the heaven described
in other sections of the New Testament.

Far more important are these words John had heard:
"Behold, the dwelling place of God is with man.

He will dwell with them,
  and they shall be his people,
    and God himself will be with them."

Recall also Jesus' words spoken in the upper room:
"In my Father's house are many mansions.
  I go to prepare a place for you.
  And if I go to prepare a place for you,
    I will come again and receive you to myself,
      That where I am, there you may be also."

These two passages give the most
    satisfying answer to the question:
Where shall we be?
We shall be with God.
We shall be with the Lord.
No concept of heaven can be any higher than this.
Heaven is that perfect communion with God
    for which we long so many times
        in this earthly life,
            but which is always far from reality.
To be at one in our wills and desires
    and thoughts and actions,
        to have nothing within
            which separates us from him
                even to the least degree, this is heaven!

No concept of hell could be more horrifying
        than the opposite:
                to be completely separated from God
                        in an existence in which he has no part,
                                in which those values that
                                        make up his character and person
                                        are altogether foreign.

Where shall we be in the life everlasting?
We shall be with God.
More than that we need not know.

Then what shall we be like?
The creed gives answer in the words
        which speak of the resurrection of the body.

We think of our spirits as having perfect communion
        with God, who is spirit.
Yet somehow we feel this
        would not be quite enough.
It is impossible for us to imagine an existence
        without some kind of body,
                for it is through our bodies
                        that we give expression to ourselves.

The creed affirms this feeling of our need.
Our existence in the life everlasting
        will not be as disembodied spirits.

Paul indicates that we will have bodies,
 though not the same bodies.
They will be different.
He writes that now we have perishable bodies;
 then they will be imperishable.
Now we have bodies of weakness;
 then we will have bodies of power.
Now we have physical bodies;
 then we will have spiritual bodies.

These differences will be welcome.
They will not be for the worse but for the better.
These are not inferior qualities,
 but superior qualities.
So we will be fit for a higher life.

Now a final question: what shall we be doing?

We can be assured of certain general
 characteristics of life after death.

Actually we have already seen glimmers of these
 when the creed speaks of
  the holy Catholic Church and
  the Communion of Saints.
The Church Universal exists both
 on earth and in heaven.
A part of its life is the communion of saints.

We human beings are made for fellowship,
    not only with God,
        but with other human beings.
This is one of the highest joys of life,
    one of life's richest experiences.
Heaven will not be poorer, but richer.
Thus the communion of saints must be a part of it.

Someone once gave a very sensible answer
    to the question: "Do you believe
        we will recognize our loved ones in heaven?"
He replied: "Do you believe we will be more stupid
    in heaven than on earth?"

The best things of this earthly life will surely
    be continued on a higher level.

Another of these continuances surely will be work.
This is a part of the life of the church universal.
The opportunity to serve God, which is now ours,
    will be continued.

Jesus' parable of the talents
    is a strong indication of this.
After their Lord's return, the faithful servants
    were given back their talents, and more,
        with the command to continue
            serving their Lord.

We are promised rest of a kind, yes.
But rest is not a matter of doing nothing.
The desire to be useful is a part of us,
    both now and then.

"We shall rest, and faith, we shall need it,
 Lie down for an eon or two,
 Till the master of all good workmen
 Shall put us to work anew."   [unknown]

Again the Scriptures indicate over and over
    that a very essential part of human life is worship.
You may say: "Well, to worship through eternity
    as I worship here is not the greatest thing
        I can imagine."
However our worship here is but a shadow
    of perfect worship.

Sometimes, even in this life, we know moments
    when we acutely feel the presence of God.
Think how it would be were all
    moments of worship like those.
So they will be in the life everlasting!

Now here, perhaps, is the right place for us
    to recognize the fact that
        as we think of the life everlasting
            or just one element of it, say worship,

we may be prone to say:
how monotonous!

We should realize that the emphasis
of everlasting life is on quality
rather than on quantity.
And the quality affects the feeling of quantity.

The legend is told of some monks
in a certain monastery
who were troubled
about this very matter,
whether life everlasting
might not be boring and tiring.

One day, one of them, Brother Antonio,
wandered away from the monastery,
following a brook in its course.

"When suddenly a low, sweet vibrant note
Smote on the brother's startled ear;
A sound so sweet flung from so fair a throat,
As never mortal man did hear."

Antonio stood enraptured.

"Hours fled like pulsebeats in that feast of bliss.
And still the monk, alert, untired,

Afraid a single of those notes to miss,
Drank in the sounds, divine, inspired."

But at last they ceased, and brother Antonio
    became conscious that the whole day was gone
        and the evening was at hand, and he must hasten
            back to the monastery.

When he arrived there, to his surprise,
    he found that everything had changed.
Not only was the monastery different,
    but the monks were different, too.
He did not know them, and they did not know him.

"At last, he cried—'I am Antonio,
    At Matins I my cell did leave,
    To spend the day afield; and now I know
    Not whence this sudden change at eve!'"

"'Thy name,' an old monk cried, 'Antonio?
    I read the tale this very morn
    Of one who left a thousand years ago,
    Beloved of all, ne'er to return.'"

Antonio was astonished.

"'A thousand years,' he cried, 'spent like a day
    In listening to young warbler's song?

Thank God! Let heaven's joy be what it may,
It ne'er will tire, ne'er be too long!'"

"And as he spoke, the sturdy, ancient frame
In crumbling atoms fell apart,
And tenderly the wondering brethren came
To bury him with prayerful heart."

The quality of life everlasting transcends all time.
Even in this life, at rare moments we experience it.
Much more shall we do so after death.

"So will the peace which simple faith does give
Steal o'er my heart and calm my fears.
Teach me below the endless life to live
And taste the joy of endless years."

I believe in the Life Everlasting.

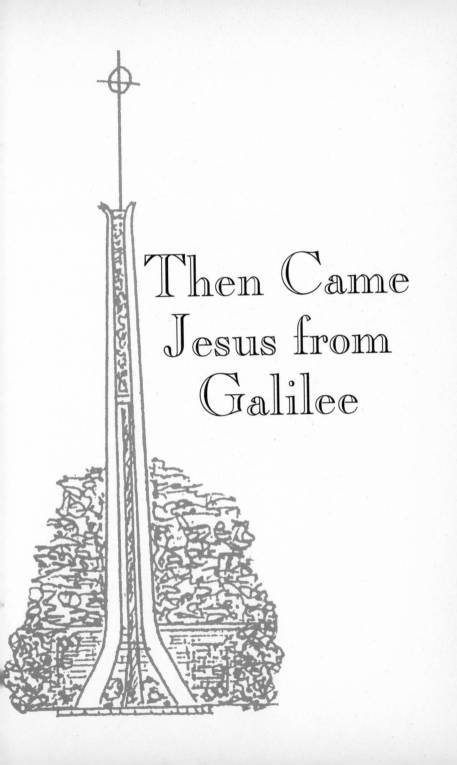

Then Came
Jesus from
Galilee

Then Came Jesus from Galilee

Matthew 3

Baptism

The promises had been on record for centuries.
    Someday the seed of woman
      would crush the serpent's head.
    Someday one would come,
      the servant of the Lord,
        through whom mankind would be redeemed.

In the fullness of time a child was born
    and laid in a manger cradle in Bethlehem.
Thirty years passed for him in Nazareth,
    where he reached maturity in body, mind, and spirit.

If the promises were to be fulfilled in the man Jesus,
    something must happen, and soon.
He must accept God's mission for himself.
He must leave Nazareth.
He did this in his baptism.

Jesus' baptism was not the same
    as the sacrament we know.
Since this was instituted by himself,
    we must see it as something else.
It was an event in which certain new relationships
    were being established.

In it he was accepting God's servant-mission for him
    as his own and was consecrating himself to it.

John's baptism, which Jesus received,
    was one of repentance.
The most pressing meaning of the repentance
    John preached was that of turning.
His plea was to turn to the Kingdom of Heaven,
    to choose it over any former way,
        to set out to live a new kind of life beneath God.

This Jesus did.

In his baptism he was deliberately choosing
    a new way of life over the old.

The old way had involved learning,
    growing, receiving.
The new way included giving.

The old way had been lived
    under the authority of the Nazareth home.
The new way would lead away from that
    and would even mean opposition to it.

The old way had centered
    around one kind of work, carpentry.
The new way would be the new work
    of a traveling teacher and preacher.

The old way had been one in which
    his unique powers were veiled.
The new way would mean using
    those powers to end suffering and sorrow.

The old way had been one of obscurity and silence.
The new way meant being the center
    of attraction and controversy.

He was initiating a drastic change in his life.
He was putting the Nazareth years behind,
    replacing them with years of servanthood.

In the baptismal event he was changing forever
    the relationship he had with other people.

Though the major meaning of repentance
    as preached by John

was a turning from the old to the new,
there was present also a note of purification.
There was a recognition of sin.
There was a desire to be cleansed.

We do not believe Jesus needed these.
Yet, what he would do from this point on
was strongly related to human sin.

The heart of his mission was to save his people
by identifying himself with them,
bearing their sins.
In his baptism he was symbolically
becoming one with them.

Jesus had not come to condemn,
to stand aloof in his purity which none denied.
He had come to enter fully into human life:
to eat and drink with publicans and sinners,
to suffer with them,
even more, to suffer for them.

His baptism was the initiation of that process.
Though he was not to share their guilt,
he was to bear their guilt.
This part of his life was to be
the predominant note of his ministry.

In the baptism event a particular relationship
  was established with the Father.

What meaning this part of the experience
  must have held for him!
What if he was wrong in the conclusions
  he had drawn in those thirty years?
He had come to know of God's Messiah.
He believed himself to be that one.
What if he were wrong?

What if the course of his life, as he saw it,
  and to which he had consecrated himself,
    was not the way of the will of the Father?
What if this identification with his people,
  rather than the aloofness
    of the other religious leaders,
      was not the way to accomplish his mission?

But there was present in the experience
  the Father's approval of those first thirty years,
    and of that which he had done that day,
      of the concept of the mission
        which he held, and to which
          he was giving himself.
There was the consciousness of that approval
  through the words, "With him I am well pleased."

And there was a new empowering for the mission.
Now he could say with a sure knowledge and confidence:
   "The spirit of the Lord is upon me,
      because he has anointed me
         to preach good news to the poor.
   He has sent me to proclaim release to the captives,
     and recovering of sight to the blind,
       to set at liberty those who are oppressed,
        to proclaim the acceptable year of the Lord."
This was the announcement of his mission
   as he had conceived it,
   as he had consecrated himself to it.
He was at that very moment ordained
   by the laying on of God's own hands!

We must now ask if this conscious leaving
   of Nazareth by Jesus has meaning for us.

We must remember that Jesus' life
   is a pattern for our lives.
We must remember that his mission
   is still our mission,
     if we are truly his body.

We must also realize that Nazareth years
   are vitally necessary, that the term represents
     a time and a means for growth,
     a time when faith reaches full flower.

On our way, study and meditation and worship
    cannot be left out of the Christian's life.
We must also know that for us to remain
    in the Nazareth of the church pew,
        or the private closet, will mean certain failure
           even as it would have been for Jesus
             had he remained in Nazareth.
During our Nazareth years and experience,
    certain commands and a way of life
        are placed before us.
Their fulfillment demands our leaving Nazareth
    to give where we have been receiving.
We hear in Nazareth years words such as these:
    "Seek first the kingdom of God."
    "You are witnesses of these things."
    "If anyone would come after me,
        let him deny self,
           and take up his cross and follow me."
    "Go into all the world."

The realization must strike home that this is for me!
This eternal call and summons which sound in my ears
    must be my call!
Now I must consciously follow it.
Now I must consecrate myself to it.

I must enter a new life.

I must leave human authority behind
   to follow that which is divine.
I must release powers
   which have been hoarded for myself.
I must leave obscurity for my voice
   and my life to speak for him.

With these decisions made,
    I must then arrive
       at a means for their fulfillment,
          realizing it cannot be reached
            by standing aloof from humanity.
Like Jesus, Christians must choose
   to enter the lives of those they would serve
    in the name of Christ.
Our Lord lived with those he taught.
He brought healing to the broken-hearted
   by sharing their pain.
Entering their captivity, he freed them.
He knew the bruises of humanity, not by hearsay,
   but by feeling their pain in his own suffering.

So the Christian must follow him,
   entering the life of humanity and
     becoming a living channel
       through which God's salvation
         may enter their lives.

As the call is accepted,
    as the means is determined
        in accord with God's will,
            there will come that which Jesus knew,
                the experience with God
                    which authenticates the fact
                        that here is a true child of God
                            who has accepted the mission
                                to which God has called him.
And there will come then God's anointing
    with the power for its success.
And there will come the words:
    "With him, with her, I am well pleased."
Nothing higher can be desired by the Christian.
Nothing higher can be given or received.
But it will never come until one leaves Nazareth.

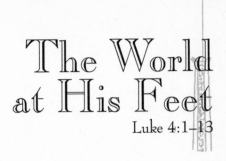

The World at His Feet

Luke 4:1–13

Temptation

Jesus had been set apart
    for his servant mission at his baptism.
But how would he go about doing the mission?
What means should be used in its accomplishment?

With this decision to be made,
        how understandable that he should be led
            into the wilderness for a period of forty days.

This was a very real decision he faced.
Scholars may differ as to whether the account
    of his temptation is to be taken literally or spiritually.
But there is no difference of opinion
    as to the reality and intensity of the experience.

He must decide between several ways and one way.

One of the ways would be to bring the world to himself
    through a ministry to the physical needs of humanity.

We cannot think the temptation to turn the stones
    into bread was only a temptation
        to provide food for himself
            during the forty days or the three years.

His dedication was such that it involved small concern
    for his own livelihood.
He was thinking of humanity, not of himself.
If he satisfied the need of human beings for food,
    surely he would draw them to himself.
Such have always turned to and followed those
    who have held out a promise of relieving hunger.

Why should Jesus not use his powers to provide
    bread for the world?

Because it is never enough to feed the body.
This is a lesser need of humanity, not the greatest need.
A person may have everything in the world
    in the realm of material possessions.
But unless he rightly uses what he has,
    he is more dead than alive.
His table may be groaning beneath the weight
    of the banquet while his spirit starves.

He may have bread for the years of his earthly life.
But what is that when his body has returned to dust?

What would it be for Jesus to save his people
    from physical death unless he could save them
        from that which destroys the spirit?
His way, then, must answer the highest need,
    not the lowest need.

His way must save them, not from starvation,
    but from separation from God.
His way must save them from their sins.

Not that Jesus was unconcerned with physical hunger.
He showed on more than one occasion his awareness
    of the hunger of the crowds.
Not that he would have his followers be unconcerned
    with hunger in the world.
Not that he would not lead us to do whatever we can
    to answer that hunger.

It was rather that he would set his mind and heart toward
    humanity's deepest need and longing,
        communion with his Father.

There was another way to bring the world to his feet,
    the way of conquest.

This is the way which has existed all
     through the centuries of human history.
Gather together an army of strong men.
Equip them with the best and most modern weapons.
Supply them with brilliant leadership.
Cross border after border.
Conquer, conquer, land after land, people after people,
     until all are subject to the conquering hero.
Jesus' own people had known this pattern all too well:
     Tiglath Pilesser, Nebuchadnezzer,
          Cyrus, Alexander, Ptolemy, Caesar.

As for Caesar, was not the world at his feet
     at that very moment?
True, his foot was forcing the world into the dust
     of submission.
But did the world worship at Caesar's feet?
There is a difference in kneeling
     at the feet of another because one wants to
          and because a spear is pressed into his back.
Once the pressure of the spear is eased,
     the captive ceases to respond.
He revolts.

This has never been God's way.
His desire has always been that men and women
     kneel before him freely.

God wants sons and daughters,
    not slaves groveling in the dirt.

Jesus' way must be another way, the way of love.
No knife at the throat, but the force of love.
Such a force will hold through torture and sacrifice.
Such a force will lead through darkness and peril.

Such a force will travel over mountain and sea
        that love may become a part
            of the lives of others.
Jesus' way must be this way.
There was yet one other way to bring the world
        to his feet: the way of spectacular exhibition.

Why not go to Jerusalem,
    climb to the peak of the temple,
        throw himself toward the ground
            before the astonished eyes of his people?
Surely his Father would save him.
The result would be overwhelming.
Both leaders and people would kneel before him.

But it would not last!
The spectacular soon becomes commonplace.
Once the impossible is done,
    we human beings demand something more.

When some of us were children,
    the greatest feat we knew was Lindbergh's flight.
How wonderful!
He was the hero of our generation.
But forty years after, when a movie was made
    of his story, the producers found it necessary
        to send a delegation throughout America
            explaining to those who would listen
                the significance of that flight.

Jesus' way would be different.
His spectacular feat would be different,
    for that which is hideous and horrible,
        that which is degrading,
            such as a man dying in agony on a cross,
                attracts attention.

Those who pass by ask: Why is he here?
And the answer is given: He is here for you!
"If I be lifted up, I will draw all people to myself,"
    he said.

This is the costly spectacle he must become,
    not a cheap spectacle in the temple courtyard.
This has never lost its magnetism.
This has never become commonplace.

This has never lost out to demands
   for a greater display.
There can be nothing greater.

To bring the world to his feet was his purpose;
     not for honor and glory that might come to himself,
       but that the way might be opened for all
         to come to his Father.
His way would not be the way of turning stones
     into bread, but the way of his broken body,
       that humanity might feed upon the bread of life.

His way would not be the way of force
    by which he would place a crown of power
      on his head and compel submission.
It would be the way of love which would permit
    a crown of thorns and a cross
      to draw all people to himself.

His way would not be the way
    of cheap and easy spectacle,
      attracting attention for the moment.

It would be the way of love's being lifted upon a cross
    with magnetism strong enough
      to draw the whole world to himself.

The world at his feet?
Yes, he wanted that,
     that the world might kneel at his Father's throne.
But his feet must walk a bruising and a wounding way.

Many ways to choose,
     but only one way would he choose,

"To everyone there openeth
A way and ways and a way,
And the high soul climbs the high way
And the low soul gropes the low.
And in between, on the misty flats,
The rest drift to and fro.
But to everyone there openeth
A high way, and a low.
And everyone decideth
The way his soul shall go."

So Jesus chose.
So we call him Savior and Lord.
So we are redeemed.
So we receive power to walk his way with him.

Mountain and Valley

Luke 9:28-36

Resurrection

Jesus had never told his disciples who he was.
He had never told them what he must do.

At length, through watching him,
    listening to him, feeling for him,
        they had come to understand who he was.
"You are the Christ, the Son of the living God,"
    they said.
Only then did Jesus take the next step
    of telling them what he must do as the Messiah.
From that time he began to show his disciples
    that he must go to Jerusalem and suffer many things
        from the elders and chief priests and scribes,
          and be killed, and on the third day
            be raised from the dead.

But the twelve were not ready for the idea
    of death and resurrection.

"God forbid, Lord, this shall never happen to you;
     you are the Messiah.
          It cannot be for you to suffer and be killed.
               You misunderstand the way you are to go."

Still Jesus insisted, and more,
     telling them this must be their way also
          if they would follow him.

Both the disciples and Jesus had their minds made up.
There was a conflict here which could not be resolved.
Although they remained together physically,
They were miles apart in understanding.

The days which followed must have been the saddest
     in Jesus' life, six days of loneliness.

He had chosen these men to follow him,
     but not one of them fully followed him now.
They loved him and he loved them,
     but they were poles apart.

Ahead were his days of suffering,
     and they were incapable
          of the fellowship of suffering.

At this point, then, he called three of them,
     Peter, James, and John,
          and made his way with them to a nearby mountain.

There he knelt to pray, and, as they watched,
    he was transfigured before them.
What this means exactly we may never know.
But at least this:
    That the glory of his divine sonship
        shone through the veiling flesh of his humanity.
    His face was like the sun,
        and his garments became white as light.
His disciples sensed the presence of God's men of old.
Somehow they heard God speaking to them:

    "This is my beloved Son with whom
        I am well pleased.
            Listen to him!"

The connection between Peter's confession
    of a few days before and this new happening
        cannot be missed.

At his baptism Jesus had received the Father's
    affirmation of himself and his mission.
Now the disciples were receiving the Father's
    affirmation of their confession as to who he was.

This was not for Jesus' benefit.
It was for them.
"You are right, Peter, James, John.
You are right!
He is the Messiah, the Son of the living God!"

But this, so far, had only to do
    with who he was,
        not with what he was to do.
The old conflict remained.
The old feeling persisted.
It was voiced by Peter:
"Lord, it is good to be here.
This is how it really should be.
I will make some shelters,
    and we will live here in this place of peace and joy.

This is how it should be for the Son
    of the living God."

Joy and glory, not suffering and death!
This is how it should be for his followers.
Enough of this talk of denying self
    and shouldering crosses,
        of suffering and death!
Surely they were right.
He had been wrong!

But remember the voice!
Not only did it affirm to the disciples who he was.
It also affirmed what he must do.

"Peter, listen to my son.
If you know who he is,
    also know that he understands his way.

If you confess he is the Son of God,
    surely you must have confidence
      in what he says.
Listen to him, Peter."

Listening to him meant
    they could not remain in that place of glory,
      the glory they sought for both him and themselves.
Listening to him meant they must go down
    into the valley below.
Down in the valley was humanity.

Down there, instead of Moses and Elijah,
    were a distracted father and his very sick son.

Down there, in place of the reassuring voice
    from heaven, was the crowd
      complaining about the ineffectiveness
        of the other disciples.

Down there, in place of the light of divine glory,
    was the darkness of human need.

Down there, instead of a light leading
    toward heaven, was a road leading
      toward Jerusalem and Golgotha.

"Peter, listen to my Son!
  He must go down.

Go down with him.
Enter his life of cross-bearing.
Your experience on the mountain will shine
     through the darkness of the valley.
But your life is down there, not up here!

Listen to my Son!"

You and I know something of Peter's problem.
We confess with him that Jesus is the Christ,
     the Son of the living God.

But, where Peter rebuked Jesus
     for seeing the cross ahead
          and going toward it, we do not.
We are thankful he went down from the mountain.

We, with hindsight, do not argue with the way
     by which he became the Savior of the world.

But argue with him we do about the way
     of Christian discipleship,
          changing Peter's words only slightly.
"Yes, Lord, you go down in the valley,
     walk the way of suffering and death.
          Redeem us, Lord, and all humanity.
We will wait here until you return.
We will worship each Sunday in peace and beauty
     where the rude sounds of the world
          cannot intrude.

We will have our devotions behind the closed doors
    of our rooms where the cries of race and clan
        cannot be heard."

But to take up crosses is not for us!
We will remain in our sanctuaries,
    in those places of safety
        we have made for ourselves.
Ah, but if we follow this way,
    we will have missed what Peter
        and his friends finally did!
For they did listen to him.
They did go down into the valley with him.
They did not understand it all.
But they went with him.
No, not all the way for a time.
Much of their following was at a distance.
They stood in the shadows as he suffered and died.
But at least they stood and watched,
    until three days had passed,
        until the living Christ stood with them again,
            until he called them anew to follow him,
                to be his hands and feet and voice
                    in the world, even though
                        it would mean their suffering
                            and death.

This time they heard.
This time they followed all the way.
Call the roll of their names, and let tradition answer:

James . . . killed by a mob in Jerusalem.
Matthew . . . slain by a sword in Ethiopia.
Philip . . . hanged in Phrygia.
Bartholomew . . . flayed alive in Armenia.
Andrew . . . crucified in Achaia.
Thomas . . . run through by a lance in India.
Thaddeus . . . shot to death with arrows.
Simon . . . crucified in Persia.
Peter . . . crucified in Rome.
Matthias . . . beheaded.
Only John escaped a martyr's grave!

A right fair record for men who refused
   at first to go all the way with Jesus,
      wanting only glory and light, peace and rest.

But they had seen the cross,
   a risen Lord,
      his love,
         his mission,
            and made all these their own.

This can happen to us also, you know.
The very same things can yank us
   out of our sanctuaries
      and make us walk his way,
         making us into extensions of him,
            ministering to the bodies, minds,
               and spirits of humankind.
It is the way the Master went.
Should not the servant tread it still?

Some Near Jesus

Some Near Jesus

Here and there one sees the twelve disciples
    depicted in stained-glass windows in churches.
There they are in splendor and beauty and serenity.
All about them is an atmosphere of peace and light
    that this particular art medium conveys.

But these are stained-glass figures.
Take these men out of their windows,
    place them together as living persons,
        and what kind of atmosphere would prevail?

We often think of the disciples singly.
We forget they were brought together
    for three years by the call of Jesus
        and lived together night and day.
What kind of a group was this?
How did they act and react to each other?

They were not, as individuals, any more fit
    to be subjects of stained-glass windows
        than any other people.

They were very real human beings,
    with great faults as well as great virtues.
Another insight is that bringing together
    these twelve men who would—and did—irritate
        each other was a ridiculous exercise
    if one expected the group
        to accomplish anything.

They formed an ideal arena for all manner
    of discord.

Place Simon the Zealot beside
    Matthew the publican.
Simon was a super-patriot, a fervent nationalist.
Nothing rankled him so much as did the fact
    that he and his people were subject
        to a foreign power, Rome.
He was a member of the Zealots,
    a group which carried out
        a constant harassment
           of the Roman authorities.
Any means was permissible
    if the purpose was advanced.

Another term for the Zealots was the Assassins,
    or as we would say, the Terrorists.

On the other hand, Matthew
    was a collaborator and sympathizer
        with the Romans.
Even more, he gave himself actively
    to maintaining their system
        by collecting taxes for them.
So he had become an outcast from his own people.
He was barred from worshiping with them.

He was barred from almost all Jewish
    civil and ecclesiastical responsibilities.
He was not one a good Jew would want
    to have in his home on a social occasion.

How can we see these two living with each other
    for even a day, much less for a period of years,
        eating at the same table,
            walking beside each other,
                sleeping in the same room?

Or, place Peter and Thomas side by side.
Peter was one whose actions were ruled by impulse.
How many times is he seen making
    some snap judgment which demanded
        a resulting strong commitment,
            or taking some course of action
                brought about by
                    a hastily made decision?

He was usually the first of the twelve to speak out.
"Who do you say I am?" Jesus asked.
Peter immediately responded for all of them,
        "You are the Christ, the Son of the living God."
But look at Thomas.
Thomas was a man with a practical mind, a realist.
His procedure was to think
        through everything carefully,
                weighing this against that,
                        balancing pros against cons
                                before arriving at a conclusion.

No decision could be based solely
        on the emotions of a moment.
Hard, cold facts must be the prologue
        to commitment.

"Only if I can see his wounds
        and place my hands in them
                will I believe he is risen from the dead."

It takes small imagination to picture
        the constant rub of these two on each other,
                Peter being always exasperated
                        by the slowness of Thomas:
"Oh, great fishes, here we go again!
Won't he ever make up his mind?"

And Thomas dreading every moment
    what Peter might do next,
        fearful of the impulsiveness
        of this natural leader,
            wary of what Peter's actions
                might mean to himself.
What a conflict there must have been
    because of the working of their different minds!

Or, take John and surround him
    with all the others except James, his brother.
Remember, he was a young man,
    about eighteen when called to discipleship.
He was set in the midst of older men,
    this overly ambitious youth.
To make it worse, he was seemingly closer
    to Jesus than the others.
We know the results of his ambition and
    his closeness to Jesus when he asked Jesus
            to give him the place of honor
        and privilege in the kingdom.
When the others heard of it,
    a cloud of suspicion, distrust, and disgust
    settled over the whole group.

And there was another unattractive facet
    of his character, his temper.

He and his brother were called
    Sons of Thunder.
"Shall we call down fire from heaven
    to consume them?" John asked Jesus
        when the Samaritans refused them hospitality.

Don't you know others of the twelve
    received similar tokens of John's affection
        through the years?
So this member of the twelve had many traits
    which surely rubbed the others the wrong way
        time and again through the years.
And they had to put up with him.
We could go on and on with these men,
    placing them beside each other
        to see how they got along.

Put Judas Iscariot there.
He was the only one of the twelve from Judea.
All the others were from Galilee.
How did this Southerner, with his strange accent,
    get along with the eleven Yankees?

Or note the fact that some of them
    were most likely far better off financially
        than others, Peter and Andrew,
            James and John, for instance.

The point is this:
It is almost inconceivable that anyone,
    setting out to do anything,
        and seeking a group of persons
            to learn and follow through on it,
                would bring together such men who,
                    by their very personalities,
                        held such seeds of dissension.
Surely the enterprise would be doomed
    before it even got off the ground!
Yet this is exactly what Jesus did!
And this is exactly what he still does in his church,
    wherever there is a congregation
        of God's people called to live and work
        and worship together.

There are those with strong political differences,
    poles apart as were Matthew and Simon.
There are those with strong emotional
    and intellectual differences,
        whose thought processes are no more alike
            than those of Peter and Thomas.
There are those who are as self-centered
    and quick-tempered as John.
There are those from different parts
    of the country or the world,
        with different accents,
            backgrounds, and cultures.

There are those of different ages, social positions,
    and economic conditions.
There are those with differing theological positions
    and ways of looking at the Scriptures.
And all are present within the church,
    called by Christ, just as were his early disciples.

We know, however, that, despite their differences,
    the little band of disciples not only survived
        those years, but also accomplished
            their assigned task
                with astounding success.
It was not that they were softened up
    and jammed into a common mold,
        though they did change in some ways.
It was, rather, that they managed to live
    and work together despite their differences.

This was possible because of the One
    who was at the center of their individual
        and collective lives.

Because he called them to himself,
    as they came to him,
        as they became rooted in him,
            they were held together by something
                far, far greater than those factors
                    which pushed them apart.

There were disagreeable situations, yes.
There were uncomfortable times, yes.
But their commitment to and love for Jesus
    was stronger than their incompatibilities.
Their unity in him was greater than their diversity.

Which must be true of his church in every age.
We who compose it are, let us admit it,
    all frail human beings.
We are not and never will be look-alikes,
    act-alikes,
        think-alikes,
            and live-alikes,
                all differences erased.

But, when our allegiance to the one we call Lord
    is what it should be,
        we will be held together by bonds
            which differences cannot sever.

When we are one with him, a special relationship,
    greater than ourselves and our differences,
        exists with each other.

No force of disintegration within us
    can destroy this.

If we love him as individuals,
    we will live together in unity as his people,
        to the glory of our Father God.

Joseph

Matthew 1:18–25

The most prominent figure in the nativity scene
  is the baby Jesus.
Next is Mary, his mother.
Last in prominence in the scene
  of this small family is the man Joseph,
    always in the background.

When we see Joseph in the gospels,
  we are told that he and Mary were betrothed,
    promised to each other in marriage,
      yet not married.

We can easily see how Joseph spent his spare time
  in the interval between their betrothal
    and marriage.
The small house in Nazareth had to be prepared.
Furnishings had to be made.
Surely Joseph's sensitive touch went into each
  piece, enhanced by his love for Mary.

Then came the day Mary told Joseph
   with hesitation that she was with child.
Imagine his shock and bewilderment.
Even after her explanation of the origin of the child,
   that he was the Son of God,
      it must have been no better for him.
He wanted to believe her, but he was human.
   He could only believe the worst.
The betrothal must be terminated.

Yet he could not bring himself
   to expose her to public shame.

He would do what must be done privately,
   with only the two required witnesses.

But then, as he drifted into troubled sleep one night,
   an angel appeared to him in a dream, saying:
"Joseph, son of David,
   do not fear to take Mary your wife,
      for that which is conceived in her
        is of the Holy Spirit.
"She will bear a son,
   and you shall call his name Jesus,
      for he will save his people from their sins."

Joseph knew the course he must follow.
Instead of ending the betrothal,
   he would marry Mary.

Instead of public shame and private whispers,
    there would be dignity for Mary.
And for the child there would be a name
    and an earthly father.

So it was.
In all this Joseph revealed himself
    as a man of faith and love, a man of faith in God
        and God's revelation,
            a man of love for this maiden.
So in obedience to his vision,
    Joseph assumed the awesome responsibility
        placed upon him, and from this point
            he seems to blend into the background.
But not really.
For all the major decisions
    regarding Mary and the child were his to make.
He determined Mary should go with him
    to Bethlehem for the enrollment
        ordered by Caesar Augustus.

With what consternation he tried
    to find a place in Bethlehem
        for Mary to stay.
And always he was there,
    keeping watch in the shadowed background,
        as shepherds and wise men held center stage
            with the holy child and his mother.

What were Joseph's thoughts?

Armand Currie has thought something like these:

"Joseph was only a carpenter.
He knew nothing of the world outside
    the realm of his own little sphere.
He only knew how to work with wood;
    how to make toy wagons for little boys,
        and wooden dolls for little girls,
            and yokes for oxen; how to rebuild
                rickety old benches
                and tables and beds.

How could he be expected to rear and train
    the child to become the Savior of the world?"

What fears were his!
How real his fears proved to be as
    again in a dream he was told:
"Rise, take the child and his mother,
    and flee to Egypt,
        and remain there till I tell you;
            for Herod is about to search
                for the child, to destroy him."

So Joseph's was the responsibility
    of protecting the little family
        as they fled through the darkness of night
            toward the ancient land of their fathers.

His was the task of building a new life
in an alien land until Herod was dead
and they could return to Nazareth.

We know from the way things were
in that culture and time that Joseph's role
was by no means secondary.
Often we think the chief influences upon Jesus
were his mother Mary
and the village synagogue.
These were factors, surely,
but we cannot forget Joseph!
The father and husband in a family
was the priest of his household.

He presided on such great occasions
as the feast of the Passover.
He patiently taught the children
the meaning of the heritage of Israel.

He was the one whose responsibility it was
to teach the Torah to his sons.

Whether we like it or not,
the Jewish religion was a man's religion.
It was passed on from father to son.
There can be little doubt that Joseph fulfilled
his spiritual responsibilities equally as well
as he had fulfilled his other responsibilities

during the time of danger in Bethlehem
and the flight to Egypt.
It was a man's obligation to teach his son
some time-honored trade,
working with the soil, or metal, or wood,
or goods to be sold, or nets and boats.
So the trade of father was passed on to his son.

Someone has pictured Joseph as teaching Jesus
much more than the mere process
of working with tools upon wood,
using this experience to teach him
about people something like this:
People are like wood.
Some are bent and crooked, made so
by the fierceness of the winds
and storms they endure.
Some are coarse, others fine-grained.
Some are hard, others soft.
Some are strong, others weak.

Many are easily broken, but all are good
and need only to be fashioned by a master hand
to become what God intended them to be.
All they need is one who can take the tools
of love and patience and mercy,
and make them strong and straight and whole.

So the silent years passed by,
    until at the age of twelve Jesus' first recorded
        words when he was seemingly
           lost in Jerusalem.
Sought in desperation by his family,
    and found in the temple, Mary asked him:
        "Son, why have you treated us so?
           Your father and I have been looking
           for you anxiously."

And Jesus' reply:
    "How is it you sought me?
        Did you not know that
           I must be in my father's house?"

Jesus was speaking now, you understand,
    of a father other than Joseph, his known father,
        just as he was to bring in the word "Father"
          over and again in future years,
            not only in speaking
              of his Father God,
           but teaching all people to think
             of God as their Father.

Have you realized what this says about Joseph?

There are some human fathers
    who are such that the most blasphemous thing

about God which could be told
    to their children is that
        God is their heavenly Father.
Who would want God to be like
    some human fathers?
But Joseph had been such an earthly father
    to Jesus that the best Jesus could teach
        about God was that God is a heavenly Father!
What this says of Joseph's fatherhood,
    of his love, his goodness, his care,
        his desires for his children!
In this father who was not his father,
    Joseph's son, who was not his son,
        found a concept great enough to hold
            this tremendous idea of God!

Though we hear of Mary on through the gospels,
    this scene in Jerusalem is the last
        in which we see Joseph.
We can only assume that Joseph died sometime
    between this point in Jesus' life
        and the beginning of his public ministry.

But what a heritage Jesus had received from Joseph.
How well this man who had been chosen by God
    had fulfilled his overwhelming responsibility.

If the average person were asked to name
    those who had counted the most
        in the life of our Lord, Peter, Andrew, James,
            and John and the others would be listed.

But really, the most important man in Jesus'
    earthly life was the first man in his life
        who in courage and faith and love
            filled a role most would have declined
            from the very beginning.

Joseph who has been forgotten so many times
    through the ages, should be held up
        as an example of fatherhood,
            and God should be thanked for the man
            who was father to a child
               who was not his son!

Peter

Luke 5:1–11
John 21:1–19

It began where it was to end.
    It was to end where it began.
        Beside the sea.
            With a boat.

I had seen and talked with Jesus before.

He had told me,
    "Though your name is Simon,
        you will be called Peter."

Now he was where I was mending my nets.
He had taken over my boat
    to separate himself from the crowd around him
        as slightly offshore, seated in it,
            he taught them.

When he had finished,
    he told me and my fellows
        to push out into deeper water
           and let our nets down.

117

When we did,
      there was such a catch of fish
            as we had never seen before.
"I will make you catch men," he said.
And then, "Follow me."

I did, leaving behind my whole life:
      my family, the boat, the nets, the village.
That was how it began.

For three years I was with him,
      watching, listening.
Certain times in those years stand out in my mind.

There was the day he asked those closest to him
      who we believed him to be.

I answered for all:
      "The Christ, the son of the living God."

Then he told us
      he was going to Jerusalem
            where he would be arrested and killed.

This did not fit my confession.

This could not be for the Christ.
This could not be for the Son of the living God.

I argued with him.
>until he told me to stop tempting him
>>to take some other course.
I did.

But I still believed what he said must happen
>could not happen.

I was even more sure of it
>another time that stands out in my memory.
The day he took two others and me
>to the top of a mountain where, as he prayed,
>>his face lit up as the brightest of lights.
We could see other figures with him.

We could hear a voice
>affirming what we believed about him.

Overwhelmed, I proposed that we stay
>there forever on the mountain
>>in that place of glory and light.

But he would not hear of it
>and led us back down the mountain,
>>back into life,
>>>his face set toward Jerusalem.

Then came that period of time of a night
    and two days and another day.
We were gathered around a table
    for the Feast of the Passover.
Jesus spoke again of what was coming and more:
    that one of us would betray him,
    that all of us would desert him, and
    that before the cock crowed three times,
      I would deny him three times.

"No, Lord! I will never desert you!
    I will never deny you!"

But it happened just as he had said.

All of us fled into the darkness
    after he was betrayed with a kiss.
And I, in the courtyard below the room
    where he was being held,
      I, accused by some of being one of his
        followers, denied with curses
          from my old fishing days
            that I even knew him!

I heard a rooster's crow,
    and Jesus, being led away, turned
      and looked into my eyes.

And, oh, the look!

I left, went off by myself, and wept bitterly.
I was not even there when they crucified him.

Darkness fell.
The sun rose on a day of despair,
    and set on a night of despair.

I had believed he was the Christ.
What had happened to him
    could not have happened to the Christ.

I had been wrong about him.
Still I knew he was the best man I had ever known.

He had been friend and companion and teacher.
    I had loved him.
    I had denied him.
And he had died knowing what I had done.

Ah, but then the next day's dawning and rumors
    from the graveyard that he had risen,
        and a command through a "young man"
            at the tomb to the two Marys:
"Go tell the disciples and Peter."

Why this?

Did he no longer look on me as one
        of his disciples?
Or, was it that he thought I would no longer
        think of myself as being included in the group,
                and he wanted me to know I was?

He came to us in the locked room that night,
                but there was no special sign or word to me.
Was I one of his or not?

I knew I did not deserve to be.
I knew I was of no use to him any longer.

And then it ended where it began,
        on the seashore, back in Galilee fishing,
                a voice and a figure seen dimly
                        through the morning mist.

"Let down your nets, men!"

They were filled as they had been once so long ago.
I knew then, it was the Lord.

Throwing myself into the water,
        I half waded, half swam, ashore—
                and stood before him
                        while the others brought the boat in.

No word from him to me.
Red-faced, I stood there in silence,
    not knowing what to say,
So saying nothing.
Then the others were there
    and breakfast was eaten.
And he called me aside.

"Simon," (The old name before he had called me)
    I was back where I had been before
        he had given me the new name,
            Peter. (Rock)

"Do you love me more than these?"
    (The fishing things of the old life?
        The other disciples?)
"Yes, Lord," I answered,
    "you know that I love you."
"Then feed my lambs."

"Simon," (a second time)
"Do you love me?"
    (Not more than these, but simply love)
"Yes, Lord, you know that I love you."
"Tend my sheep."

"Simon," (a third time)
"Do you love me?"
    (Not simply love, but even love)

I felt my heart would break.
Three times I had denied him.
Three times he had asked me if I loved him.
"Lord, you know everything;
        you know that I love you."
"Feed my sheep."

Then he added, as three years before: "Follow me."
Though I had denied him, he would take me back.
Though I had denied him, I was still his.
Though I had denied him, he could still use me.

So I remind you now:
        after he had first called me,
            I who had confessed him to be the Christ,
                the Son of the living God,
                    had deserted him, had denied him.
You may also, sometime, somewhere, somehow.

If and when you do,
        afterward--
            as you are by the silent seashore,
                or out in a field,
                    or in a deep forest,
                        or on a high mountain,
                            or in the stillness of your room,
                                he will find you
                                    and ask his question of you:

"Do you love me, really, really love me?"

I want to be sure you know
    when he does, he asks in love.
I want to be sure you know
    when he asks, if you but answer:
        "Lord, you know everything;
          you know I love you,"
            he will respond with love
              as he did to me,
                "Come with me, follow me,
                  feed my sheep,
                    feed my lambs."

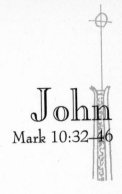

John
Mark 10:32–46

There was little lovable about the man.
Oh, there might have been.
For John was the youngest
    of the twelve nearest Jesus,
        and often there is unusual affection
           for the youngest member
              of the family or team.

But how the others must have bitten their tongues
    and ground their teeth at times
        in the presence of John.

John was an ambitious young man.
We see this in his coming to Jesus
    with James, his brother,
        to ask for the most important place
          in Jesus' kingdom.
How the others must have resented youth shoving
    forward to seek recognition
        and honor and power.

There were one or two things
    which made the request appear reasonable
        as John saw it.
He must have been the wealthiest of the twelve,
    along with his brother.

His father, Zebedee, had been established
    in the fishing trade for years
        and had prospered in it.

The request must have seemed reasonable also
    in that he and Jesus were probably cousins,
        his mother most likely being
            the sister of Jesus' mother.
Often members of a leader's family
    have preferred positions in the organization.

What better candidate could present himself
    to Jesus than himself?
Perhaps none.
But there was nothing here
    to make the others love him.

He was a man with a violent temper.
This comes clear through one incident in particular.
The direct route from Galilee to Jerusalem
    led through Samaria.

The Jews and the Samaritans
    wasted no love on each other,
        having carried on a bitter feud for centuries.
The Jews claimed, as was true,
    that the Samaritans were no longer
        pure-blooded.
And they claimed that the religion
    of the Samaritans had been contaminated
        through the centuries.

Why, they worshiped on a mountain in Samaria
    rather than in the temple in Jerusalem.

On his last journey to Jerusalem,
    Jesus took this short route.
He sent some of the disciples ahead
    to make arrangements for an overnight stay.

But all doors were closed to them
    and hospitality was denied them.

John's reaction to this was violent indeed.
"Lord, will you have us command fire
    to come down from heaven
        and consume them?"

For this reaction, Jesus called John "Boanerges,"
     Son of Thunder: explosive, hair-triggered,
          ready to denounce and condemn
               fellow human beings
                    with no thought whatsoever.
Evidently this was not an isolated display
     of John's temper.
Once would not have warranted such a nickname.
This must have been one instance of many,
     and was not a characteristic
          which would endear him to others.

He was also a man of great intolerance.
One day, away from Jesus,
John came upon another man
     who was casting out demons
          in the name of Jesus,
               seemingly with some success.

Obviously the man was not one
     of Jesus' close disciples.
And John, in a display of intolerance,
     ordered him to stop the work of healing
          in which he was engaged.

To John, the name of Jesus was copyrighted,
     and a stranger had no right to use it,
          even in a good cause.

But Jesus, hearing of it, commanded John:
"Let him alone.
He who is not against us is for us.
He is doing the same work we are doing.
Then he must be on our side.
Leave him alone in his ministry."

So there John was:
    a young man of arrogant ambition,
        of violent temper,
           of supreme intolerance.
"Son of Thunder," he was indeed,
    with constant rumblings and lightening bolts
      as everyday occurrences of his life!

How very, very remarkable, then,
    that this Son of Thunder is known to us
      as the beloved disciple, the Apostle of Love.

There is some discussion as to who was
    the actual penman of the letters of John.
But there is no doubt that either John or one
    of his close associates in later years
      was the actual penman, so that the spirit
        and mind and heart of John
          were behind and in
            and through the letters.

Remember the man of ambition
   in the light of these words:
"If we confess our sins, he is faithful and just,
    and will forgive our sins and cleanse us
      from all unrighteousness.
If we say we have not sinned,
   we make him a liar, and his word is not in us."
Here is a man who no longer judges his worth
  by his possessions or kinship,
    but who sees himself as one
      who deserves nothing
        and yet, by the grace of God,
         has received all things.

He would be the very last to seek any position
  of honor in the kingdom,
    desiring no place greater
      than the least of his fellows.
Remember the man of the violent temper
  who would call down fires of destruction
    on his fellows, in contrast to John,
      the Apostle of Love:
"He who loves his brother abides in the light.
But he who hates his brother is in the darkness
  and walks in the darkness."
And again:
"We know that we have passed
  out of death into life,
    because we love the brethren.

Anyone who hates his brother is a murderer.

By this we know love,
    that he laid down his life for us;
        and we ought to lay down our lives
           for the brethren.
Little children, let us not love in word or speech
    but in deed and truth."
Or there is the old John of the intolerant heart
    now saying:
"Beloved, do not believe every spirit,
    but test the spirits to see whether
        they are of God.
Beloved, let us love one another,
    for love is of God,
        and he who loves is born of God
           and knows God."

For him, now, there is but one test
    of a true follower: that his love for others
        authenticates his confession.
The intolerant, resentful heart is dead.
There is, in place of it, a genuine respect for
    and love for everyone whose work
        bears the mark of the love of God.

The Son of Thunder became the Apostle of Love
    as his characteristics were redirected
        under the lordship of the Lord of Love.

Jerome wrote that the aging John, highly respected
    as the only apostle still living,
        was invited to preach
           in the church at Ephesus.
His coming was widely publicized
    and on the appointed day
        a great crowd assembled,
           filling every available space.

When John arrived,
    he was so feeble that he had to be carried
        into the building.

After eloquent words of welcome
    and a lengthy preparatory service,
        John was lifted to his feet to speak.
A great hush came over the congregation.

Everyone strained to hear each word
    of this man who had been so intimately
        associated with Jesus
           in his earthly ministry.

The old man spoke:
"Little children, love one another,
    love one another,
        love one another."
He sat down; his sermon was over.

Many went home disappointed.
They shook their heads and said:
　　"Too bad! The old man's in his dotage.
　　　　Why doesn't he stop trying to preach?"
But others realized that simple as
　　the apostle's sermon may have seemed,
　　　　it spoke of a transformed life.
It speaks to us anew:
Little children, love one another!
Be what each of us is intended to be
　　under the Lordship of Christ,
　　　　not sons or daughters of thunder,
　　　　　　but apostles of love!

Andrew

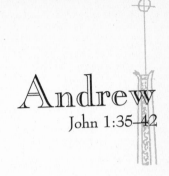

John 1:35-42

When the names of the twelve disciples
    are listed, Peter is always first.
Andrew is listed second
    with the note that he was Peter's brother.

When the gospels were written,
    it was assumed that everyone
        would know who Peter was.
He had been the natural leader of the twelve.
He had been in a place of prominence
    in the life of the early church.

So, when Andrew's name was mentioned,
    it was quite natural to throw in the fact
        that he was Peter's brother.
Then he was identified.

So Andrew was one of those people destined
    to go through life being identified
        by someone else better known than himself.

He was not quite important enough in his own right
    to be easily recognized by the readers
        or hearers of the gospels.
Yet, in his gospel, John tells of three incidents
    which make Andrew a man to remember,
        clothing him with a character
            other than his kinship to Peter.

The first of these was at the very beginning
    of Jesus' ministry.

At that time, Andrew and John were disciples
    of John the Baptist.
As they stood with him one day,
    Jesus passed nearby
        and was immediately identified
            to Andrew and John by the Baptist
                as the one they were really seeking,
                the Messiah.
"Behold the Lamb of God."

At which Andrew and John left their old leader
    and went up to Jesus and asked him
        where he was staying.
"Come and see," was Jesus' answer
    and invitation to them.
This they did, remaining with him
    through the night,
        listening to him and asking questions.

Early the next day Andrew went
    and found his brother, Simon Peter,
        and told him:
            "We have found the Messiah,"
                and brought him to meet Jesus
                for himself.

The second incident John records took place
    some time later.
A great crowd had been listening to Jesus
    many hours, with the time
        for the noonday meal long past.

The disciples expressed their concern
    for the hunger of the people,
        feeling they had some responsibility
            since their teacher had preached so long.

Then Andrew came forward with a boy
    and told Jesus:
        "Here is a boy with five loaves and two fish."
Of course this would not help much.
But at least Andrew brought the lad
    to Jesus with his lunch.

The last incident took place in Jerusalem
    before the crucifixion.
A group of Greeks had heard of Jesus
    and were eager to talk with him.

They approached Phillip,
    perhaps because of his Greek name,
      with their request:
        "Sir, we would see Jesus."
One would suppose that Phillip
    would have taken them immediately to Jesus.
Instead Phillip went and found Andrew,
    told him about the Greeks,
      introduced them to Andrew,
        and then, with Andrew in the lead,
          took them to Jesus
    where Andrew performed the introductions
    and paved the way.

This is all the information there is about Andrew
    aside from the fact that he was Peter's brother.

Does Andrew come through
    with any special characteristics?
Yes, indeed!
One thing ties all three incidents together
    and is amazingly significant.

In each of these incidents,
    Andrew brought someone to Jesus.
Was this important?
Look again at each incident.
Andrew went and found his brother, Peter,
    and brought him.

This brother became the leader of the twelve,
  and later of the early church,
    until the rise of Paul.
Had Andrew never done anything but this,
  he would be a man to remember.
For in a sense, everything Peter became
  and did must be credited to Andrew.

Was it important that a boy
  who had five loaves and two fish
    was brought to Jesus?
Was it important that a crowd be fed?
  Not really.
They would not have starved to death.
And Jesus indicated that people placed
  too much emphasis on being fed.
Far more important was the teaching of Jesus
  to which this experience led.
    "I am the bread of life."
Had Andrew done nothing more than open the way
  for this teaching of Jesus,
    his contribution to Christianity
      would have been far from small.

Was it important that some Greeks,
  an inconsequential number
    of unimportant people,
      have an interview with Jesus?

Well, when all was discouragingly dark for Jesus,
    when the week of his suffering was underway,
        he was enabled to look beyond that time
           to the peoples of the world
              who would become a part
                of the kingdom.
When his own people were beginning to reject him,
    here were some who were seeking him.
Though the cross was near, and death,
    here was a brief vision of an hour of glory.

If no more was accomplished at that moment
    because of Andrew, our Lord
        had a moment of encouragement.
And of course, aside from these measures
    of the importance of Andrew's acts,
        there is the importance to God
           of each of these persons
              involved in these experiences,
                and the fact that all of them
                  were placed in touch
                    with the living God in Christ,
                    through Andrew.
This in itself cannot be minimized.

One last thing.
The means by which Andrew accomplished this
    is of much importance.

Seemingly, Andrew was not an eloquent speaker.
He was not to become a great Christian writer.
Some of the other disciples would be
    one or both of these.

But Andrew led these people to Jesus
    simply because he had the capacity
        to be a friend.
In fact, if we had to describe
    this man near Jesus in one word only,
        it would have to be: Friend.

There was a fraternal friendship
    with his brother Simon.
Many brothers are friends
    through childhood and youth,
        but grow apart in the years of manhood.
Not so with Andrew and Peter.
Evidently Simon Peter was well aware
    of Andrew's search for the meaning of life.
Otherwise, Andrew would have been unable
    to tell so easily and so quickly
        of the successful end to his quest:
            "We have found the Messiah,
                John and I."
The relationship of these two brothers
    made this possible.

Then, what other than friendship
    could have enabled Andrew to bring
        the lad with his small lunch to Jesus?
How had Andrew come to know the boy
    in such a crowd?

Why had the boy been willing
    to go along with Andrew?
Andrew must have found him
    on the edge of the crowd,
        where small boys are always found
            playing and tussling.
Somehow, he had established a relationship
    with him so that the two became friends,
        and the lad was willing
            to trust this rough fisherman
                and entrust to him his lunch.
This was something worked out between friends,
        not between strangers.

Surely this was the reason Phillip
    called Andrew when the Greeks
        came seeking Jesus.
Many Jews would have turned down such a request.
Some of the disciples would have done so.
The idea! Some not of the house of Israel
    seeking an interview with the Messiah!

But not Andrew, sought out by Phillip
    as one who would welcome these strangers
      and would know what to do about them!

Andrew reminds us of that deep concern
    which we should have for those we love
      that they also have a meaningful relationship
        with the living God through Jesus Christ.

He points us to those of our families,
    reminding us of our responsibilities
      to help them, both young and old,
        toward a deeper knowledge of Christ.

He points us to children and youth,
    reminding us of the responsibility
      of every church member to aid in the nurture
        of all the children of the church,
          not just our own.

He reminds us of the strangers we meet
    in our neighbors, or at work, or our social life,
      that they, too, are intended
        to be children of God.

He points out a way for us to meet our
    responsibilities toward all of these,
      through friendships dedicated to Christ

with willingness that they be used
by God for his purposes.
Andrew had many friends.
He had one supreme Friend.
He could not be content until the many,
their hands in his, were led to place them
with confidence in the hands of Jesus.

We have friends.
We will have many more in life.
We have one supreme Friend.
Do they know each other?
And, if not, what will we do about it?

Thomas
John 20:19–29

Popular speech has not dealt kindly with Thomas.
He is called "Doubting Thomas."
To be sure there is an element of truth in that.
Yet it comes rather close to slander.
For it does not tell the whole story,
    and it does not tell us the end of the matter.

A fairer picture of Thomas emerges
    as we recall the incidents involving him
    as recorded in John's gospel.

The first of these reveals a man
    who was both realistic and courageous.

It revolves around Jesus' friend, Lazarus.
News had come that Lazarus was seriously ill.
But Jesus had done nothing for two days,
    before announcing his intention
        of going to Bethany.

Bethany was near Jerusalem
      and the Jewish authorities there
            had determined by then that Jesus must die.
Therefore, what Jesus proposed doing
      seemed to be suicidal.
Even more, word had come at the last moment
      that Lazarus had died
            during that two day period.
So it seemed Jesus' reckless proposal could
                  accomplish nothing whatsoever.

At Jesus' announcement
      that he was going to Bethany,
            the disciples seemed about
                  to abandon him to his madness,
                        until the voice of the usually silent
                              Thomas was heard:
"Let us also go, that we may die with you!"

This was not the voice of a pessimist
      who thought things were worse
            than they were, but of a realist.

Thomas knew the danger.
He felt the action could end only with death.
The fact that it did not
      does not discount his realistic evaluation.

For only two months later,
    Jesus returned to Jerusalem
        and met death by crucifixion.

The realism of Thomas' judgment, then,
    underscores his courage.
Even aware of the danger
    he spoke those brave words:
"Let us go with you."

It would be easy for an optimist to say that,
    believing the situation to be better than it was.
Yet Thomas rallied the faltering loyalty
    of the other disciples
        when only disaster appeared to lie ahead.

So Thomas reminds us of the need
    for followers of Christ to be realistic.
Less of the optimists who say:
    "There will never be difficulties
        in following Jesus."
More who will say:
    "Let us go with you anywhere."
More who know full well that going with Jesus
    will mean the death of self will.

Jesus needs more followers
    who have the courage to go with him
        despite the heavy and fearful demands
            which may be made of them.

Another incident reveals Thomas
    as a bewildered man who had grave problems
        in grasping and understanding
            what was happening.
In the Upper Room, the night of the betrayal,
    Jesus was still trying to get across to his
        followers that he must suffer and die.

"Where I am going, you know," he said,
    "and the way you know."
At this point Thomas' bewilderment
    broke through:
"Lord, we do not know where you are going,
    and how can we know the way?"

"Lord, we don't know what's going on.
Our whole world is about to crash in on us.
What we had thought would come
    is so far away and so hopeless.
Even tonight is uncertain and unpredictable.
How can we know the way?"

Jesus' answer was: "I know you
    do not understand what is happening.
But whatever happens, you have me.
What you need is not an explanation
    but my presence."
So Jesus' only answer was himself.

Just here Thomas leads us to ask the same question
    of Jesus and hear his words again.
Just as often we are as bewildered.
What's the world coming to?
What's my life coming to?
I can't see beyond the moment.
I can't answer my questions.
I can't solve my problems.

To this Jesus answers:
    "What you need is not some magical road map
      of the future with everything
        laid out for you.
What you need is the realization that
    I am the way, the truth, and the life!"

For us also it is not a matter of what is going
    to happen, but of who will be with us
      in whatever comes.

If we know that, our bewilderment
    will never overwhelm us.

Only three days later the scene is the same,
        most likely the Upper Room.
Now we see Thomas as a man
    who cannot believe in the resurrection.
Here is the basis for the idea
    of "Doubting Thomas."
After Jesus had died on the cross,
        seemingly Thomas wished to be alone.
This is how some face grief.

When Jesus appeared to the others
        Thomas was not with them.
When the others told Thomas later
        of Jesus' appearance to them,
            he refused to believe the good news.
He was no different from the other disciples.
At one point there had been just such doubt
        on the part of all of them.

When the women had come from the tomb
        to make their report,
            it seemed to all the disciples an idle tale,
                which they could not believe.
When Mary Magdalene reported her experience,
        they could not believe.

When the two who had been walking
    on the road to Emmaus raced back
        to report their experience,
            the disciples still would not believe.

Thomas was no different from the others.

Not one of them believed until he had seen
    the risen Lord himself.

"Unless I see in his hands the print of the nails,
    and place my finger in the mark of the nails,
        and place my hand in his side,
            I will not believe!"
Doubting Thomas!

But also a man of sublime faith and devotion!
For Jesus returned to the meeting place days later,
        and this time Thomas was there
    and was invited to put his finger
        in the nail prints and his hand
        in the spear-gashed side.

Confronted with the risen Lord,
    Thomas breathed out the Gospel's
        greatest confession of faith:
            "My Lord and my God!"

In the presence of the living Lord,
    doubt and unbelief were replaced
        by faith and certainty.

Thomas deserves to be called a doubter
    no more than the others.
And his confession must remove forever
    the word "doubting" from before his name.
"Believing Thomas" it should be!

Through this last incident,
    Thomas reminds us of these facts:

Jesus is not intolerant of the person
    who wants to be sure.
He did not blame Thomas for his doubt
    any more than he had blamed
        the others for theirs.
He knew once Thomas had come
    through this period, he would be one
        of his surest followers.

This does not mean that one should be content
    to live with doubt.
Thomas reminds us that certainty does not come
    so much through intellectual conviction
        as it comes through a first-hand experience
           of the presence of the risen Lord.

One last reminder from Thomas is that faith
    is most apt to replace doubt as one participates
        in the fellowship of believers.
Apart from the life of the community
    Thomas did not believe.
As he was with the others
    Jesus made himself known and stifled his doubts.

This is not to say a person
    cannot find or be found
        by Christ in solitude.
This has happened to some.
It is to say that nowhere is one
    more likely to find him and be found by him
        than in the company of others
            seeking him together.

The last glimpse we have of Thomas
    is with the others as Jesus came to them
        beside the sea of Galilee.

Thomas was determined to be a part
    of the fellowship of the believers.

The words of his great confession:
    "My Lord and my God,"
        still ringing in his heart,
            he was ready to proclaim it

to the far reaches of the earth
and even to die for it,
as tradition tells us he did.

No doubting Thomas he,
but Thomas,
man of faith
and man of courage!

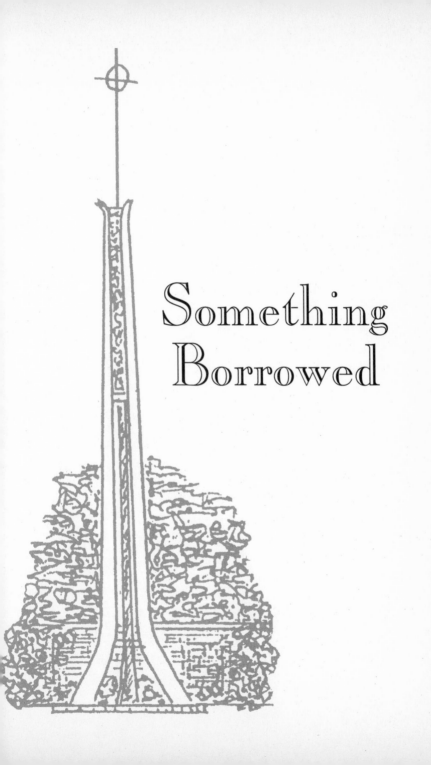

Something Borrowed

He Used My Stable

Luke 2:1–14

You don't know my name.
    History is aware of me,
        but only where I lived,
            the work I did.
Most who received my services
    called me by my work, not by my name.

"Innkeeper, give me a bed for the night.
    Innkeeper, bring supper.
        Innkeeper, stable and feed my horse."

"Innkeeper, we have come a long way;
    my wife is about to give birth,
        but there is no room anywhere in the town.
Oh, couldn't you find some place, any place,
    just for the night?"

I had filled my inn
    with the rich, the powerful,
        the religious rulers of the nation.

This last request was by a working man,
   judging by his hands and rough clothes,
      with a young wife, in the simplest garment,
         riding upon a donkey.

I had filled my inn with those others,
   so no room for these two from Nazareth,
      strangers in a strange place,
         strangers in such great need.

What could I do? What could I say?
Then I thought, why not the stable?

And a child was born,
   and he was named Jesus,
      and a star shone,
         and shepherds came,
            and the little family left.

And a man, thirty years later, with that same name.
   Jesus, crowned with thorns, I heard.
      Jesus, bearing a cross, I heard.
         Jesus, laid in a tomb, I heard.
            Jesus, alive again, I heard!

Jesus, oh, Jesus, is it you?
Do you still need a place to stay?
Come to me again!
Oh, Jesus, it is you!
Come into my heart, Lord Jesus,
   there is room in my heart for you!

He Used My Lunch

John 6:1–15

In many ways life for me as a boy of Galilee
    two thousand years ago
        was quite different from that of your
           elementary school boys and girls of today.

When we wanted or needed to go somewhere,
    we didn't ask to be taken in a car.
We walked or we ran.

When we were at home at night
    we had to find something else to do other
        than watch television or play computer
           games.

But in many ways, life for me was very much
    like yours.
I went to school and learned to read and write.
I had to go, and I hated to get up in the morning.
And sometimes, seated near my rabbi or teacher,
    my mind would drift away
        to what I would do
           as soon as school was out.

It could be fishing, climbing the hills, or swimming.
  We played games as you do, some with a ball,
    though, instead of using bats,
      we used our hands.
We had games we played inside on rainy days,
    with boards and different pieces we moved
      like you move checkers.

But the greatest excitement in life
    had to do with crowds of people
      who gathered when and where
        something big was happening.
What it was really didn't matter.
But we were always around whenever
    there was something to attract a lot of people.
We paid little attention to what the grown-ups
    went for.
We hung around on the edge of the crowd,
    running and chasing each other
      and wrestling on the ground.

This was the way it was one day when I was eight.
A man named Jesus had been traveling
    about our land.
Everybody was talking about him,
    the things he did and the things he said.

So when word came early one morning
    that Jesus was only a few miles away,

some of my friends and I got the idea
of following the people going to see him.

Mother said I could go, and,
knowing how far it was
and how long it would take,
fixed a lunch for me,
some small biscuits and some dried fish.
I hung these from my waist in a small bag,
and I was off.

My friends and I followed the crowd.
Sometimes we got behind as we chased off
into a field or played in a stream.
Sometimes we got ahead and stretched out
in a shady place to rest,
waiting for the people to catch up.

At last the grown-ups from our town
joined with others around a man seated
on a large rock
while he talked to them.
I watched and listened for a bit just to be able
to say when I got home that I had seen Jesus.
That would be something to brag about!

Then I drifted off to the edge of the crowd
where my friends and I continued
chasing each other,
shouting and laughing.

There I ran headlong into a big man,
    tall and sun-burned, who grabbed me
        to keep me from falling down.

He did not yell angrily at me
    as many would have done.
Instead he talked to me awhile in a friendly way.
He found out where I lived, what my name was,
    what I was doing that day,
        and what I thought of the crowd.
And somewhere in our talk, I told him
    about the lunch Mother had fixed for me.
He told me his name was Andrew.

Then he asked me if I would like to meet Jesus,
    and he took me through the crowd to a place
        where Jesus was talking
            with several other men,
                apart from everyone else.
Andrew and I paused, listening to what
    they were saying about how the thousands
        there might be fed,
            for it was lunch time and all were hungry.
One suggested sending to a nearby town for food.
But another said that would cost too much,
    far more than they had.

Then my new friend, Andrew, joined in.
        "There's a boy here with five small pieces
                of bread and two fish.
But that wouldn't feed many people," he laughed.
Jesus turned and looked at me,
        with questioning eyes.
                I knew he was thinking that
                        this was my lunch, not theirs.

I answered by taking it from the bag at my waist
        and holding it out to him,
At least it would be enough for him.
And I wasn't very hungry myself.

Taking it, he smiled at me and thanked me.
        Then he thanked God as my father did at home.
Telling the men with him to seat the crowd
        in groups, he began to pass
                from group to group holding my lunch,
                        and giving some
                                to one person in each group,
                                        who then passed it to others.

I stood there watching in amazement.
Surely he would be back,
        saying my lunch had run out.
But he kept on, moving from group to group.

He didn't return to where I was until
    he had gone to everyone.
All had received something
    and all had eaten.
I could hardly believe what I had seen!
You may ask me what happened that day
    when Jesus used my lunch.
        To this day, I really don't understand.
That night at the supper table when I told about it,
    Mother said what had happened was a miracle,
        that somehow, in Jesus' hands,
            my five loaves and two fish lasted so
        that there was enough for everyone
            to eat.
Father said what had happened was that
    Jesus told each group that a small boy was
        willing to share his lunch with them,
            and that one by one,
            many in the crowd took out their lunches
                from where they had hidden them,
                    and began to share with others.

Father said that would have been a miracle too,
    for people are not often that unselfish.

Whatever happened was a miracle.
All I know is what I tell you:
    Jesus used my lunch, and everyone was fed.

Well, that was long ago.
And as I come to you across the centuries,
    I see that things are not so very different
        in your world.
For people all over the world are still hungry,
    boys and girls and men and women.
And I know Jesus, who was concerned
    about hungry people then,
        is just as concerned about them now.
And I come to you across the years
    and would take you to Jesus
        just as my friend Andrew took me.
And as we stand beside him,
    I would say to him what my new friend
        said to him then:
"Here is a boy;
    here is a girl;
        here is a man;
            here is a woman;
who has some food, but surely not enough
    for all these starving people."

And as I say that, I see Jesus turn and look at you
    with the same question in his eyes.
        "Will you place what you have
            in my hands?"

If you say "yes," I believe with all my heart
    that a miracle can happen again as it did then.
      I cannot explain how.
Maybe it will increase as it passes through
  his hands, those hands which made all things.
Or maybe the miracle will be that one by one
    others all over the world
        will put some of what they have
            into his hands,
                and the result will be that the world
                    will not be as hungry as it was.
Miracles can happen!
So come along with me, won't you?

"Lord, here is a boy, a girl,
    a man, a woman
        with five loaves and two fish,
            but such a small amount cannot feed
            all these hungry people."

Listen!
Jesus replies. "It is enough!"

He Used My Water

John 4:7–15

You ask who I am.
I am a woman.
I am a woman means I am nothing.
I cook and clean, draw and bring home water.
I bear and raise children.
This is my place.
I am no more important than a stick of furniture.
Only more useful.

I am a Samaritan woman.
We Samaritans live surrounded by
    the descendants of Abraham.
We are that, too.
But generations ago our ancestors intermarried
    with those who were not,
        and so we are a mixture,
            both physically and religiously.

The children of father Abraham, the Jews,
    will have nothing to do with us.

They go miles out of their way to avoid our land.
    And if they do have to travel through,
        they go as quickly as they can.
Going to the well is something women do together.
When it is cool, they go, visiting,
    enjoying each other's company,
        sharing the news.
But this was not for me.
I was alone in the heat of the day drawing water.
Because, well, how shall I put it?
Because I lived around.
You know what I mean.
Even Samaritans have morals,
    and I was ostracized by the others.

So there I was that day, my jar filled,
    ready to leave,
        when a shadow fell across me.
And looking up, I saw a man, about thirty,
    a stranger, from his looks a Jew.

Whoever he was, he would pay no more attention
    to me, a woman, than to a stone wall.
This was how it was.

But this was not how it was!

For he asked me for a drink of water.

I was so startled at his even speaking to me,
    much less that he would drink from a container
    I use, that I gave him a drink.

Then, overcome by the incongruity of it,
    I burst out with a question:
        "Sir, how is it that you, a Jew,
            ask me, a woman of Samaria,
                for a drink of water?"

He knew what I meant.
He knew such a thing just wasn't done.
But he didn't answer my question.
Instead, he made a statement:
"If you knew who had asked you
      for a drink of water,
          you would have asked him,
             and he would have given you
                some even better, living water."

Something about this made me uneasy.
One cannot always say what causes such a feeling.
All I can do is describe what I felt.

And I had the feeling he was taking me
    where I didn't want to go.
I had the feeling he was moving from a discussion
    about ordinary water to something far deeper.

I had the feeling he was about to make some
        demand of me that I wouldn't want
                to concede.
I had no desire to get involved with him
        in this sort of discussion.
You know how it is.
Someone, who would not ordinarily do so,
        calls you on the phone or drops by your house.
You ask instinctively: "Now what does he want?"

You throw up your defenses.
You back away.
You steer the conversation in some other direction,
        hoping he won't be able to get it back
                on that track.

So, there was something about this man
        that made me feel that way,
                something appealing about him, but
                something that made me want to avoid him.
Something that made me want to stay,
        but something that made me want to run away.

I stayed, but my mind and heart started running.
My flight took the form of a question.

Had I not wanted to run,
        I would have asked the natural question:
                "What do you mean by living water?"

I asked something else, pointing out
   how impractical his offer.

"Just how would you do this, sir?
   You have nothing to draw with.
      And anyway, are you greater
         than our father Jacob
           who dug this well?"

Almost ignoring my question, he moved on
   in the direction he had been going.
"Everyone who drinks water
   from this well
      will soon be thirsty again.
        But whoever drinks
     of the water I give
        will never be thirsty again.

What I give will continue
   to spring up within
      and flow with eternal life."

I knew now how I could get away from him.
I would make him put up, or shut up.
I knew he couldn't give me water of any kind.
When he failed, I would be free of him.
So, half facetiously, and yet,
   somehow half meaning it:

"Sir, give me this water that I may not thirst,
        that I will not have to come here ever again
                to draw water and carry it home!"
Looking at me in a curious way,
        ignoring my request,
            he instead gave a command:
"Go, call your husband and come here!"

"I have no husband," I replied.

And he said:
"You are right when you say
        you have no husband,
            for you have had five husbands,
                and the man you are living with now
                        is not your husband."

Now I really panicked!
I was in too deep with this man!
He was getting into something I always avoided,
        myself and my life.

I had no intention of going any further.
        I had to get away!
                I would get away from talking about myself
                        by talking about religion in general.

I would flatter him a bit, pretend to listen,
  then leave.

But at least I would be off the subject of myself.
"Sir, I see you are a prophet, knowing all about me.
I have often wondered, and you can answer.
Where is the right place
    to worship God,
      on this mountain
        as we Samaritans do,
          or in Jerusalem
            as you Jews do?"

That ought to do it!
But it didn't.
To my dismay, I realized he could see right
  through me.
To my dismay, he refused to get caught up
  in this popular controversy,
    and instead of talking about
      where God is to be worshiped,
        spoke of the God to be worshiped
          and of those who worship.

"God is a spirit, and the hour is coming
  when true worshipers
    will worship him in spirit
      and in truth."

Somehow he had turned it back on me again,
   as to how I worshiped,
      as to whether or not
         I was a true worshiper.
Well, I would end it right now.
I would point out that I was waiting
   on a real authority.

"Someday," I said, "one will come
   to answer all our questions.
      He is called the Christ.
       I will wait for him."

And his reply?
"I who speak to you am he!"

And so he was!
And so I tell you each one:
   "Come to him whatever your needs may be,
      and he will give you living water
         and you will never, never thirst."

Indeed, he says even more:
"Come unto me all you
   who labor and are heavy laden,
      [in any way], and I will give you rest."

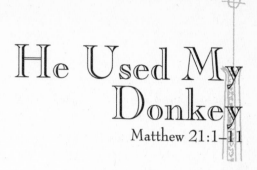

He Used My Donkey

Matthew 21:1–11

You have no reason to think I was one
    of Jesus' unnamed disciples.
All you know about me is that I lived
    outside Jerusalem
        and that I owned a donkey.
This last meant, however, that I was
    fairly well-to-do in that time,
        since a good animal such as mine
            was worth several hundred dollars.
And I had two.

You may wonder why
    I let my donkey and colt go that day
        when two strangers came
            to where they were tied and,
                without so much as a by-your-leave,
                began to untie them.

Quite naturally, I asked just what
    they thought they were doing.

One answered me: "The Lord has need of them."

I knew who they meant when
      they said the Lord.
They were speaking of Jesus of Nazareth
      whose name was on every tongue in the land.

If we had had newspapers, television,
      and radio news in that day,
            reporters and photographers would have
                  been assigned to travel with him
                        so everyone in the land knew
                              what he was doing and saying.
He was that prominent.

Perhaps you can understand, then,
      why I let the colt go.
After all, if word came to you
      that the president was near your town
            and needed the use of your car for awhile,
                  you would let him have the use of it,
                        even though you did not
                              support him.
In the same way, when this one
      of whom it was claimed
            that he was our national Messiah
                  sent for my donkey and her colt,

I had no objection since
　　I was told they would be returned
　　　　immediately.

So two men led them away,
　　and I followed along with others
　　　　who had been watching to see
　　　　　　what would happen next.

At length we came to the place
　　where Jesus was waiting.
Some of his men placed their coats on the donkeys
　　and helped Jesus get on the back of the colt.

Then they moved slowly along the road
　　which wound through the hills
　　　　around Jerusalem,
　　　　　　his disciples following on foot.

As they caught sight of the city,
　　the temple gleaming in the sunlight,
　　　　they broke into a shout:
　　　　　　"Blessed is the King who comes
　　　　　　　　in the name of the Lord!"

They broke branches from the trees along the road
　　and placed them in the path.

As we came nearer the city,
    another crowd came out from it,
        made up of pilgrims who had come
            to Jerusalem for the Feast of the Passover.

They had heard the talk in the city
    about the Nazarene.
When word came that he was coming
    into Jerusalem that day,
        they went out to see him for themselves.

Before they knew it,
    they, too, were caught up in the demonstration,
        joining in placing branches in the roadway,
            and lifting their voices in the cry
                familiar in the sacred writings:
"Hosanna! Blessed is the King
    who comes in the name of the Lord!"

So Jesus used my donkey to ride into Jerusalem.

Now of course I could see,
    as could all good people of the Hebrews,
        what Jesus was saying in his actions that day.

This was the way it had been promised
    God's Messiah would come.

Jesus, by filling the role as it had been foretold,
　　was saying for the world to know: "I am he!"
He was entering Jerusalem just as it had been
　　promised the king would do,
　　　　in majesty and triumph.

You may think the procession was something
　　to laugh and joke about.
It might appear to you to be a rather scruffy parade!

But, you see, for us a donkey was an animal
　　often ridden by kings, those of royal lineage.

So we understood that the words of prophecy
　　were being fulfilled:
"Behold your king is coming to you
　　mounted on a colt, the foal of an ass."

But we realized later he was saying also,
　　I am a certain kind of king.
　　　　I am not a king who comes on a warhorse
　　　　as the Romans.

I come in meekness and humility and lowliness.
I come to serve, not to be served.

The appearance of the whole procession,
　　the looks and dress of his followers,

common people,
   his riding upon a colt,
      all this confirmed his servanthood.

Strangely, my donkey was a paradoxical symbol,
   a symbol of kingliness, yet also
      a symbol of a servant-king.
He was a king.
What else could one be in whom
   the fullness of God dwelled,
      the maker of heaven and earth,
         the ruler of all that is?

What else could one be whom
   we came to believe in
      and worship as God's Son?

And yet the events of the week
   which followed underscored
      his lowliness and servanthood!

For, before the week was over,
   he was betrayed, arrested, ridiculed, and beaten.

He headed up another procession then,
   moving out of the city,
      struggling beneath the weight of a cross,

nailed to that cross,
as lowly as a man can be.

He died as a base criminal.
He wore a crown on his head
as a king should wear,
but one made of thorn branches.
He was seated upon a throne, high and lifted up,
as a king should be,
but his throne was a cross.
Well, one might think, that only shows
how wrong the people were in thinking him
to be the Lord of Lords and King of Kings.
They had thought him that on Palm Sunday.
They had to think otherwise on Friday.
He could not be both kingly and lowly,
both Lord and servant!

To which I can only reply:
Remember the Easter which was to come,
displaying a power never conceived of.
Whereas the greatest and the strongest of the rulers
of men had always been conquered by death,
he showed himself
even to be Lord of death!
Remember Easter!

So Jesus entered Jerusalem that first Palm Sunday
        riding upon my colt.

Again you hear the cry:
"Hosanna in the highest!
  Blessed is he who comes in the name
        of the Lord!"

And you hear the prophet's summons:
"Behold your king, coming to you humble
        and mounted upon a colt!"

You hail him as your King, you call him Lord
        still, more than two thousand years afterward.
You say he has the right to rule over you.
And that is so.

And before this week is done you also
        will hail him anew as your Savior,
                who came to serve and to give his life
                        a ransom for many.

Before the week is over you will remember
        the events of Thursday and Friday.
But then you will look beyond them
        to the great triumph of Easter,
                where his Kingship will be affirmed anew.

That day you will sing:
    "Ride on! Ride on in majesty!
    Hark! All the tribes hosanna cry;
    Oh Savior meek, pursue thy road
    With palms and scattered garments strowed.

    "Ride on! Ride on in majesty!
    In lowly pomp ride on to die;
    Bow thy meek head to mortal pain,
    Then take, O God, thy power, and reign."

And so it was.
And so it is.
And so it shall ever be!

He Used My Cross

Matthew 27:27-37

On that great point of Africa in the Mediterranean
    was the city of Cyrene.
A third of its population was Jewish,
    many of whom traveled the thousand miles
        to Jerusalem each year for the Feast
           of the Passover.

I was among those pilgrims one year
    and was drawn into an incident
        which has had more effect upon human
           history than any event of any time.

My name is Simon.

Unable to find lodging in Jerusalem
    because of the crowds,
        I stayed in one of the outlying villages.

The morning after the feast,
    as I walked toward the center city,

the birds filled the air with song;
the sun flooded the earth
with light and warmth.
I found myself singing
the grateful psalm of a faithful Jew
who has made the pilgrimage to Jerusalem.

Then suddenly my peace was disrupted
by a mob surging through the street.
At its center were Roman soldiers
striving to maintain some semblance of order.
In their midst were three men with crosses.
Despite the uproar, I heard the name Jesus
and linked it with one of the prisoners
whose face and bearing showed he had
endured far greater pain than the others.

The marks of closely drawn bonds
were on his wrists.
The back of his robe was soaked
with blood from a heartless lashing.
Down his dust-smeared face were rivulets of blood.
Their fountainheads were the thorns
of a makeshift crown.

On his raw shoulders was a rough hewn
wooden cross under which he staggered,
finally falling headlong into the filth
of the street.

All this I heard and saw.
But not for long was I allowed to stand and watch.
I was pushed into being a participant in the drama,
    forced by the soldiers to carry the cross
        of this condemned and fallen man.

From going in one direction,
    filled with one purpose,
        I was made to go the opposite way
            with an entirely different goal.
Thereby my life was changed forever!

You ask:
    Where were the thousands he had fed?
    Where were the lepers he had healed?
    Where was Lazarus, raised from the dead?
Where were those who had vowed
    to die with him?
Why were none of them carrying his cross?

I cannot answer.

You ask:
    Why was I chosen from all the onlookers
        to take up his cross?
    Was it because I was a stranger,
        and none objected
            to my being pressed into duty?

Was it because I was not a born Jew,
    but a proselyte?
Was it because my skin was African dark?
I cannot answer.

All I know is that his cross
    was placed upon my back,
        and I was driven with it,
            stumbling through the streets.

You ask: Did Jesus say anything to me? No.

But something passed between us:
    a look between one who had borne
        so many burdens for others and myself,
            the only one, as far as is recorded,
                who ever carried a burden for him.

Oh, yes, something happened
    on that frightful journey
        to my heart, my mind, my soul.

Later accounts tell of my sons,
    prominent in the church in Rome years after.
Surely you must know I told them over and again
    how I bore the cross of Christ to Golgotha.

Now, has it ever struck you
    that mine was the very service

Christ's church is to give
through the ages?

Christ's body fell beneath the weight of the cross.
And I was called to step in to carry it for him.

Is this not what his church is and is to be doing?

The church is his body.
It is given the task of doing what he would do
were he still physically present.
His spirit is strong and willing,
but he must have a body to bear the cross
and willing to do so.

The church is meant to carry the cross
to the world by word and by deed.
I, Simon of Cyrene, tell you
if the church appears to fail in your day,
it is because his body has failed.
It is because you, his hands and feet,
have not moved.
It is because you, his mouth, have not spoken.

If the church is to bear the cross of Jesus,
the individual members must;
for the body is made up
of its individual members.

All begin life as passersby.
But a different role is offered
    as you come upon the man and his cross.
You are called from being onlookers
    to being crossbearers.
Yet too many want a free ride on the cross,
    want to be carried along on it,
        rather than to carry it.

And what is it to carry his cross?

To sacrifice comfort and time in an earnest effort
    to have one's part in the church's work,
        that is to bear the cross of Christ.

To surrender talents and energy and treasure
    to be used in the church's work,
        that is to bear the cross of Christ.

To fulfill one's vocation, whatever it is,
    as a holy calling to witness to Christ day-by-day,
        that is to bear the cross of Christ.

To identify oneself with what is right,
    to stand with courage,
        to take the consequences without complaint,
            that is to bear the cross of Christ.

In all these ways one leaves the role
   of bystander, onlooker,
      to carry the weight of the cross.

The cross must be taken throughout the world,
   along every highway and byway,
      down the main street of every town,
         through every back alley of every city.

There are only two choices for anyone:
   put shoulder to it and be a crossbearer,
      or stand aside and watch it go by,
         indifferent and uncaring.

I, Simon, gave my strength to the fainting Savior.
I carried his cross to the place where he died.
Nothing else I ever did can compare with that.

One of your preachers has pointed out that
   for us all the day will come when we must look
      back to one particular act,
         the memory of which we are proudest.

When that time comes, it will not be
   the recollection of prizes we have won,
      the pleasures we have enjoyed,
         the discomforts we have escaped,

that will come flooding in
upon us with delight.
Rather, if we have denied ourselves
and borne the cross for Christ's sake,
the memory of that will be a satisfaction
with which none other can compare.
In that day we will wish the minutes
given to Christ's service had been hours,
and the hours years,
and the dollars thousands,
and that every cup of cold water
and every word of sympathy
and every act of self-denial
had been multiplied a thousandfold!

He Used My Tomb

John 19:38–20:10

Let me tell you something about myself.
My name is Joseph,
I lived in the small town of Arimathea.
I was a member of the Sanhedrin,
    the council of seventy-one men of Israel
      to whom the Romans had delegated
        the government of our occupied land.
There were exceptions to our delegated power.
Among these was that only the Roman governor
    could give the death penalty in criminal cases.

I was also a disciple of Jesus.
I was not one of the twelve, as you know,
    not even one of the many outside the twelve
      who were known as his followers.
I was a secret disciple, if there can be such a thing.

I rationalized my position
    by telling myself I could be
      of more help to Jesus

by quietly and silently remaining
on the Council rather than
by openly declaring my discipleship
and losing my council seat.

If I remained on the Council, I thought,
I would be able to influence
any future decision
when it might deal
with Jesus of Nazareth.

So I was there the night Jesus was brought
before the Council after his betrayal and arrest.
I was there as Jesus was asked:
"Tell us if you are the Christ, and also,
are you the Son of God?"

His replies to those questions
were in an idiom of our language
which clearly meant yes.

This was exactly what the Council wanted to hear.
This was all it seemed to need
to send Jesus on to Pilate with the charge
that he was openly subverting the nation
and should be executed.

Pilate examined him briefly
and then sent him to Herod.

He talked to Jesus again after Herod returned him,
  then told the Council openly
    he could find nothing
      of which Jesus was guilty.
Therefore, he would have him beaten
  and then released.
The Council was not content with this finding.
Nothing less than death would do.

It persisted in its demand for execution.
At length Pilate consented, though announcing
  it was on their heads, not his.

Let me be sure you understand.
I was there through all these deliberations.
I had thought before I would use my influence
  with the Council when the right time came.
It had come, and I did nothing.

The Council was unanimous in its decisions.
This meant, not that I had voted with the others,
  but that I had abstained.
When the "no's" were called for, I was silent.
By my very silence, I gave consent.
I did not have the courage to stand up
  and defend him!

I realized then why I had been a disciple in secret.

I had not been waiting for the right time
    to speak out.
I had been holding back because I was afraid
    of what might happen to me if I supported him!

So Jesus was turned over to the Roman guard
    for execution.
So he was nailed to the cross and lifted up
    above the earth.
So he hung there in agony.
So he died!

Overwhelmed by what had happened,
    I knew my silence had contributed to his death.

After the crucifixion I came out into the open
    as his disciple.
I had a tomb in a nearby garden
    upon which I had spent much time and money,
        preparing for my own death.

With Pilate's consent,
    I went with another secret disciple, Nicodemus,
        to the scene of Jesus' death.

While my fellow Sanhedrin members
    looked on in shocked disbelief,
        Nicodemus and I took the body

of Jesus down, wrapped it in the sheeting
  we had brought with us,
    and carried it away
      toward my tomb.
I had not had the courage to claim him in life,
  but I had claimed him in death.
I had done nothing for him in life,
  I was doing what little there was
    to do for him in death.

What was it like as we moved toward the tomb?

One of your poets of the nineteenth century
  described the feelings of a group of students
    bearing a beloved teacher's body
      to its final resting place
        on a mountain height:

"Let us begin and carry up this corpse
  singing together . . . step to a tune, square chests,
    erect each head . . .
This is our master, famous, calm and dead,
  Borne on our shoulders . . .
Well, here's the platform,
  here's the proper place . . .
    —here's his place,
Where meteors shoot,
  Clouds form,

Lightenings are loosened,
    Stars come and go.

Let joy speak with the storm,
    Peace, let the dew send!
Lofty designs must close in like effects:
    Loftily lying, leave him—
      Still loftier than the world suspects,
        Living and dying."

Our movement to the tomb was just the opposite.
With bowed heads, slumping shoulders,
    we bore our master,
        notorious, tortured, dead, to my tomb.
No joy to break for us.
No peace with the dew.

Then reports came on the third day,
    the day you celebrate as Easter,
      reports from women who had gone
        to complete our hasty work,
        reports from disciples
          who had rushed out
            to confirm what they
              had been told,
                reports that the tomb was empty,
                that the body of Jesus
                  was no longer there,

that it had been stolen
away.

Then came reports even more startling than that,
reports pointing in a different direction,
not merely that his body was missing,
but that he was alive.
Two of the disciples raced from Emmaus
to report that Jesus had walked with them
and made himself known
in the breaking of bread.

Those gathered in the room where
he had celebrated the Passover with them
were telling that he had come
to them there that night.
Those converging reports were astounding.
But they were undergirded by personal witnesses
whose integrity we had no reason to doubt,
who had been downhearted and defeated,
who had never put any confidence
in his promises to return,
who had neither the heart nor reason
to conjure up such stories.
Though Jesus had been dead and buried,
he was alive! He had risen!

He was with his followers in a way
   just as real as ever he had been
      before his death and burial.

Joy had broken with the storm!
Peace the dew had sent.

Do you grasp what all this meant?
That my tomb, now empty, was to witness forever
   to certain glorious facts?

One fact is that there is in existence
   a power greater than evil in any of its forms.

Death had always been evil's strongest weapon.
Evil had always relied on death to win out
   in its time-long struggle with righteousness.

How do you put down the best man who ever lived,
   even the perfect man? Kill!
How do you put down those qualities of love
   and righteousness he personified? Kill!
How do you end his teachings? Kill!

Evil had called up that ultimate weapon
   Friday at the cross.
But this time righteousness was not defeated
   by death!
Death was defeated by the power
   of righteousness!

Evil was conquered in my tomb.
It would continue to exist
    and make itself felt in your world
        as it did in mine.
But the outcome has been determined forever!
God and his righteousness have already won!
There is another glorious fact.
You come to it remembering this was my tomb.

It was a tomb prepared for my death.
My tomb was weak and frail, it could not hold him.
Neither can it hold me as I am one with him!

Your grave is weak and frail.
As Jesus said, because I live, you shall live also.
Since you are one with him, neither can it hold you.

If God is for us, who can be against us?
We are more than conquerors
    through him who loved us.
For I am sure that neither death, nor life,
    nor angels, nor principalities,
        nor things present, nor things to come,
            nor powers, nor height, nor depth,
                nor anything else in all creation
                will be able to separate us
                    from the love of God
                        in Christ Jesus!

Christ is risen!
   And those I have loved and lost!
      And I with him!
         And you with him!
Thanks be to God
   who gives us the victory
      through Jesus Christ our lord!

Something Borrowed
John 21:15–19

I can remember a discussion by grammarians
    regarding the increasing use of the noun "loan"
      in place of the verb "lend."
I suppose that by now this has become permissible
    through common usage.
So no one will object if you ask them:
    "Will you loan me $1,000?" except possibly
      the person being asked.

Shakespeare knew the proper usage.
So in Hamlet:
    "Neither a borrower nor a lender be.
      For loan oft loses itself and friend,
      And borrowing dulls the edge of husbandry."
Yet if ever a person did not follow such advice,
    it was Jesus.
Somebody was always borrowing
    something for him;
      or he was always borrowing
        something for himself.

THEY BORROWED A MANGER TO LAY HIM IN
The cradle made ready in Nazareth
     was no help in Bethlehem.
 So they placed him in a manger in a stable
     which had been borrowed from
          someone who did what he could
               for some strangers
                    in an overcrowded town,
               borrowed also from the gentle beasts
               accustomed to finding there hay,
                    not a baby.
They borrowed a manger to lay him in.

HE BORROWED A BED TO LAY HIS HEAD,
     a bed in the house of Simon, the leper,
     a bed in the house of Lazarus
          and Mary and Martha,
     a bed in the house of other friends
          here and there.
Though foxes have holes and birds have nests,
     he had nowhere.
So, he borrowed a bed to lay his head.

HE BORROWED SOME LOAVES AND SOME FISH
Filled with compassion for the hungry crowd
     around him,
          having nothing with which to feed them,
               he borrowed the lunch of a small boy.

He borrowed some loaves and some fish
    to feed the crowd.

HE BORROWED A DONKEY TO RIDE UPON
Wanting to enter Jerusalem as the King
    foretold in prophesy,
        not having a donkey of his own,
He borrowed a donkey to ride upon.

HE BORROWED A ROOM ON A THURSDAY NIGHT,
    to observe the Passover Feast with his disciples,
        to institute his supper,
            to break bread and bless it and give it,
                to offer a cup.
He borrowed a room for the last supper.

HE BORROWED A GARDEN ACROSS A BROOK
        to be alone that night
        to seek his Father's will one last time.
Leaving the closely built houses of the city,
    he borrowed a garden where he might pray,
        and be betrayed.

THEY BORROWED A CROSS TO CRUCIFY HIM
    The cross had been made for Barrabas.
        They placed the cross on Jesus' shoulder
            and made him carry it through the streets
                to the hill outside,

They borrowed a cross to crucify him.

THEY BORROWED THE STRENGTH
        OF A STRANGER FROM CYRENE
When Jesus could no longer bear up
                beneath the cross, when he stumbled
                        and fell to the street,
        they borrowed the strength of a bystander,
                onlooker, and placed the cross
                        on Simon's shoulder.

THEY BORROWED A TOMB WHEN HE HAD DIED
His body was removed from the cross
        and cared for.

As he had no place to lie in life,
        he had no place to lie in death.
So Joseph's tomb was used for him
        when he had died.

Even beyond the grave he was not done
        with borrowing.
This comes clear one morning beside the sea.
He is to continue his ministry to the world,
        in the world, through borrowed lives.

8888888888888888888888888888888888888888888 stop.

"I have a people who must be cared for.
I have a flock.
I must have hands.
I must have feet.
I must have a voice,
I must have human love above all.

"With these hands and feet and voices,
    with this love, I can reach out and touch
        and tend my flock.

"Peter, I would borrow yours.
Peter, do you really love me?
Really, really love me?

Then lend me your hands, your feet,
    your voice, your heart.
Peter, do you love me!

"Tend my flock . . .
    feed my sheep . . .
        my little lambs!"

Through borrowed lives like Peter's, singly,
    or banded together
        as his people, his church, his body,

the three years of his public ministry
has continued even until now.

His borrowing way is not only in the past,
It is still his way.

He comes up beside us, each, all, where we are,
        and would borrow from us.
Not a manger for a cradle.
Not a donkey to ride upon.
Not a garden where he may be alone.
Not a cross on which to be crucified.
Not a tomb in which to be buried.

Not these, since we do not have these.
Do you have a manger, a donkey, a cross, a tomb?

But some of the things he needs we do have.
Such as bread and fish to feed the hungry. Yes!
Such as clothing to clothe the naked. Yes!
Such as means to care for the sick. Yes!

Such as a place where a stranger
        may lay his head. Yes!
Such as a cup of cold water for the thirsty. Yes!

He would, in his compassion,
　　give such as these to the world.
But since he does not have them,
　　he would borrow them,
　　　　from you, from me.

But even more than that,
　　even more than what we have,
　　　　what we are, our very selves,
　　　　　　he would borrow us.
He would borrow some of us as he did Peter,
　　to leave boats and nets behind,
　　to leave other work in the world behind,
　　to make tending his sheep our work
　　　　in some church vocation.

He would borrow some of us
　　and have us work in the world
　　　　but make our common work sacred
　　　　　　as we find ways to love and serve him
　　　　　　　　behind the desk in business,
　　　　　　　　　　in the classroom,
　　　　　　　　　　　　on the farm, or wherever
　　　　　　　　　　　　　　our everyday work is done,
　　　　　　　　　　　　　　　our everyday lives
　　　　　　　　　　　　　　　　are lived.

He would borrow some of us and have us work
    as volunteers in our community,
        in school or hospital,
           or wherever there are individuals
               or groups with special needs to be met.

He would borrow some of us
    calling us in particular ways within his church,
    calling us through the voice of his people
    to special offices,
    setting us apart to the care
        and nurture and oversight
           of his people, of his church,
               as his work is done.
He would call some of us to serve him
    within the church in other ways,
        as leaders and teachers,
           using us that others in the church
               may be prepared to do his work
               in the world.

All these borrowed folk and others
    he binds together in the work of his church
    for his ministry to the world.

He who loved the world
    and gave his Son for it,

still loves it and still gives his Son
    through those he borrows.
He would borrow us,
    and his request is in his call:
    "Follow me!"

About the Author

Murphey Candler Wilds was born in Hendersonville, North Carolina. He attended Clemson University before earning a bachelor's degree from Davidson College. He later graduated from Union Theological Seminary with a bachelor's degree in divinity, and earned a doctor of ministry degree from McCormick Theological Seminary.

As an ordained Presbyterian minister, Wilds served churches throughout the South, including First Presbyterian Church in Oxford, Mississippi. He also served as the Stated Clerk and the Pastor to Pastors in the St. Andrew Presbytery.

Now retired, Wilds resides in Oxford, Mississippi, with his wife, Mary Rose. They have two grown sons.